Lancashire's Most Notorious Murders

Written and compiled by Mike Hill and Nicola Adam

Evening Post
LANCASHIRE

at heart ♡ publications

First published in 2008 by
At Heart Ltd
32 Stamford Street
Altrincham
Cheshire
WA14 1EY

in conjunction with
Lancashire Evening Post
Oliver's Place
Fulwood
Preston
PR2 9ZA

ISBN: 978-1-84547-210-8

Printed and bound by Ashford Colour Press, Gosport.

Contents

About the authors

Mike Hill was born in Liverpool in 1970, educated in the city and graduated from Liverpool John Moores University in 1993. He started his journalistic career at the *Southport Visiter* as a trainee reporter and after qualifying as a senior joined the *Lancashire Evening Post*. Mike was named North West daily news journalist of the year in 1996 and was three times runner up for the same award. He was also runner up as the UK's daily news journalist of the year in 1997. In 1999 he joined the *Liverpool Echo* as a news reporter and the following year was commended for scoop of the year at the UK Press Gazette Awards for his work on the Alder Hey organs scandal. He is a former news editor of the *Liverpool Daily Post* and rejoined the *Lancashire Evening Post* as assistant editor in 2003. He has been the newspaper's deputy editor since 2006. Mike has written for a number of publications and is author of *Preston North End: 1954 FA Cup Final*.

Nicola Adam was born in London and moved to Lancashire as a teenager. After studying language and literature at De Montfort University she travelled the world before returning to undertake a postgraduate journalism course at the University of Central Lancashire in Preston. She started her career on the *Preston Reporter* in 1998 and was awarded runner up best news journalist in the Newspaper Society's national weekly newspaper awards in 2000. After joining the *Lancashire Evening Post* she worked as a district reporter, consumer reporter and crime reporter. In 2001 she was named the Society of Editor's North West young journalist of the year and runner up news journalist of the year. A weekly columnist for four years, she was promoted to the news desk where she was first assistant news editor and is now deputy news editor. Nicola is too young to have reported directly on any of the murders covered in *Lancashire's Most Notorious Murders* but worked on several when they were re-opened as cold cases by Lancashire Police in the early 2000s.

Foreword

FEW things set a newsroom buzzing like a big story breaking. The news desk takes a telephone call, briefs the crime reporter who confirms the tip and the whole team swings into action. Pages are cleared, reporters briefed and photographers dispatched to the scene.

The adrenaline-charged days when a major story breaks are the days when a journalist earns their spurs. Getting the story first, gathering the facts and grabbing the pictures which will define the story for months and years to come. Within hours the full, gripping details will be splashed across the front page and set the whole region talking.

Lancashire's Most Notorious Murders revisits the case files of some of the biggest stories to rock the Red Rose county in recent years. Each chapter turns the spotlight on a different murder, examining the people who carried out the brutal crimes, their victims and police efforts to bring the killers to justice. Over the years *Lancashire Evening Post* journalists have travelled the world to bring the very best coverage of the stories as they have unfolded. The evil charades weaved by the killers in a bid to evade justice, the sinister motives behind the killings plus the original photographs which illuminated the cases.

In many cases researching *Lancashire's Most Notorious Murders* meant digging through dusty boxes which have lain untouched for years. Hours were spent reading through articles which together form a fascinating historical record of crimes which made headlines not just in Lancashire, but nationally and across the globe. For some chapters that meant pulling together scores of stories written over a span of many years.

The result is a book which tells the full story for the first time of those infamous crimes which have written themselves largest in the region's criminal annals.

Mike Hill
Deputy Editor
Lancashire Evening Post
June 2008

Acknowledgements

With thanks to *Lancashire Evening Post* journalists past and present and, in particular, the reporters who covered *Lancashire's Most Notorious Murders* over the past three decades:

Paul Baldwin, Tracy Bruce, Brian Ellis, David Graham, Cerys Griffiths, Stefanie Hall, Neil Hepburn, David Nowell, Jeff Postlethwaite, Jim Potts, Peter Richardson, Charles Stewart, Christine Talbot, Bob Westerdale and the late Alan Burgess.

CHAPTER ONE

The unsolved 'Ripper Hoax' murder

Joan Harrison, Preston, November 20, 1975

ON a cold, quiet and overcast day the funeral cortege made its way along the damp road, carrying a young mother on her final journey. Just a few family members and a handful of other mourners attended the solemn 50-minute church ceremony, before driving down the road in three funeral cars and several private vehicles to commit the body of a beloved daughter, sister, lover and mother to the chilled ground of the cemetery on a murky December day. Only a pile of wreaths and bouquets, including a large cross of white chrysanthemums and red roses, brightened the final resting place of Joan Mary Harrison. The card attached said simply, "With all our love and remembrances, Mum and Dad." At the bottom, "Goodnight and God bless Mummy – Denise and Maxine."

The date was December 5, 1975, and the location was Chorley, Lancashire. The church service at St Mary's Roman Catholic Church, in Market Street, was less than one mile from the semi-detached home of Joan's parents in Millfield Road. But the dignified ceremony belied the horrific truth of how Joan died just a few miles down the road in neighbouring Preston's notorious 'Skid Row'. Little did her family know that her brutal demise was to reverberate down through the years. That nearly four decades and thousands of police hours later, it would remain one of the most debated unsolved murders in British criminal history. Because Joan was not only murdered; she may have

The funeral procession.

been a victim of one of Britain's most notorious serial killers, the terrifying Yorkshire Ripper.

The question is still unresolved after all these years. Joan may have been Peter Sutcliffe's other victim. Or did the work of a callous Ripper hoaxer lead detectives astray, obliterating the path to her real killer? Wherever the truth lies, justice has never been done for Joan, who could never have comprehended how her squalid death would create a murder hunt of a magnitude never seen before in Preston.

It all started as a young woman's previously respectable life spiralled out of control. Joan Harrison, née Riding, was a bubbly, house-proud and loving mother-of-two, who worked sporadically as a machinist and shop assistant before her life took a turn for the worse when she began drinking heavily and experimenting with drugs. Brought up by her parents in Chorley, she attended St Mary's School in the town, before moving to Preston with her first husband, with whom she had two daughters, Maxine and Denise. But life at the family home in Miles Street, near Moor Park, turned sour, the marriage broke up and her husband died shortly after.

Joan Harrison.

She began a new relationship with a much older man, 34-year-old Wilf Roach, who she lived with for eight months. But, as her descent into alcoholism and drug-use continued, that relationship foundered when Wilf suspected she was unfaithful. Soon after, Joan began falling behind on her mortgage payments on the Miles Street house and eventually lost the property.

Her beloved daughters were taken into care, one to live with Joan's mother, the other with social services. She then married Paul Raymond Harrison, a carpet fitter from Burholme Road, in the Ribbleton district of Preston. During the inquest into Joan's death, 27-year-old Harrison told how he had not lived with his wife for two years because of her heavy drinking and drugs use. In the months before her death, Joan lived at bedsits in Frenchwood Street and Brackenbury Road before beginning a relationship with her 47-year-old landlord David Keighley at East View, Deepdale.

They were due to be married the following June. He later spoke of his love for Joan and explained how he had tried to give her a stable home life, but spoke also of her terrifying drinking binges. But that was a side Mr Keighley never saw. "Joan never brought any boyfriends back here, she knew I wouldn't have it," he said. "We were very close. We were engaged to be married and I bought her a ring. She had her problems but I was trying to show her the better side of life, like staying at home at night, sitting by the fire and watching television instead of fooling around the town.

"I told her I didn't care what she had done in the past, it was now that counted. I fell in love with her and I couldn't wait to get home at night to see her. She got under my skin. I'm no drinker but she did used to have too much. She sometimes came back tipsy but she was a good tenant and I can't say a bad word against her."

Joan's elder sister Margaret Upton had seen the writing on the wall. She told the *Lancashire Evening Post* that in the last six weeks before her death Joan had become a "fleeting memory" to her sister's family. Once a regular visitor to the household in Havelock Street, Margaret's children would innocently tell her, "Auntie Joan is ill again." Margaret knew better, her sister often came to the house drunk. Warned by doctors about her failing health, Joan turned more to the bottle for solace and to ease the worst effects of her chronic bronchial asthma, which she had battled with since childhood.

Margaret said, "I knew something would eventually happen to her... things were going that way but I never thought she would be killed. It was pitiful really, the way she went. She had been a good mother and her kids thought she was great, though they were not living with her. There was another side to her so many people will never have known and she did love her kids such a lot."

> **❝ I knew something would eventually happen to her... ❞**

By 1972, Joan was plumbing the seedy depths of Preston, losing access to her children as she was unable to cope. She was dubbed "a complete wreck of a human being" when she appeared on her 25th birthday at Preston magistrates court in 1974. By the time she was brutally murdered the following year, she had already stared death in the face once as doctors battled successfully to bring her back to life in a Preston intensive care hospital bed. Joan had imbibed a cocktail of drink and drugs, triggering a massive asthma attack. She had turned blue and her heart stopped beating.

Joan was mixing with the dregs of society and spent much of her time in Preston's more downmarket pubs and clubs. She became addicted to cough mixture, which contained morphine, drinking up to eight bottles a day. Joan was unemployed and lived off social services. Her life became a living nightmare. Despite rumours she was on the game, Joan was never arrested nor cautioned for prostitution. But she was known to sleep with men she knew for "favours", whether it was booze or lodgings. She would share drinks with winos and swap small talk with the local hookers. Often Joan and some of her new low life associates would use a derelict house in Avenham where much drink was consumed. Cider, meths, whatever they could get their hands on. She was on skid row. Down and out. She had finally hit rock bottom.

Her family tried to rescue her. But she turned on them too. Her court appearance saw her charged with stealing £51 of property from her sister and forging a drug prescription, increasing the prescribed quantity from 30 to 60 tablets. Her sister said later, "She got in a terrible state and in the end I felt I had to report her."

Out of custody, things were not getting any better. Margaret put a stop to her frequent stays at Havelock Street, later saying, "I said that unless she kept going to Alcoholics Anonymous, she could not stay with me." Joan was an accident waiting to happen. But her untimely death was no accident.

On the day she died, she had been working voluntarily in St Mary's Hostel for the homeless where she had a job as a part-time cleaner, washing plates and cleaning up. It was Thursday November 20, 1975, and after finishing her shift at lunchtime, Joan went out with colleagues for a drinking session at the nearby St Mary's pub and later moved on to the pubs in the New Hall Lane area.

She was the worse for wear, or as warden Ian Finchen described her, "a little drunk", when she returned to the hostel later and needed a lie down on one of the rest beds.

He later described her as, "A kind sort of girl, good-natured as a rule. She knew quite a lot of the residents and had seen the rougher side of life. But Joan needed to drink far too much. This was the cause of many of her problems."

From the hostel, Joan returned to the home in East View, Deepdale, which she shared with Mr Keighley. Anxious to get a late-night drink, she left again at 10.20pm, walking the damp and badly-lit streets into the town centre. Ten minutes later, at around 10.30pm, wearing a light green three-quarter length coat with an imitation fur collar and brown calf-length suede boots, she was seen in Church Street. It was the last time that Joan would be seen alive.

The first sign that anything was amiss was when Mr Finchen reported her missing on Saturday morning. The following day her sister Margaret received a knock on her door that she would never forget. A policeman informed her that her sister was dead. Joan had been found battered to death in a disused lock-up garage in Berwick Road, Avenham. She was just 26 years old.

Her body was discovered lying face down in a pool of blood by mother-of-five Mildred Atkinson, who was on her way to the paper shop at 8am on the Sunday morning. Her husband, Ronald, had left only moments earlier to walk to work. But as Mildred, 47, walked along the street she had walked hundreds of times before, a gust of wind blew a wooden garage door open, to reveal the battered and blood-stained body of a young woman. She dashed to a telephone box and called the police.

On November 24, just days after the murder, Mrs Atkinson told the *Lancashire Evening Post*, "The door was blowing open and I saw the body lying face down. There was a coat over her head and I saw blood on the ground beside her. I did not know it was a woman and thought it may have been a drunk who had banged his head."

Speaking later, she said the memories of that fateful morning will always be with her. "I remember it every time I walk past that garage. I go down that street every day. It used to bother me at first. But I still remember it now."

Joan had been bludgeoned to death in a savage attack and a bite mark had been left on one of her breasts. She suffered serious injuries caused by a flurry of blows to the head, which had been covered by a coat. Her clothes laid about her in almost ritualistic fashion. She was just two miles from her East View flat. Later that week, it emerged the killer had sex with Joan before she died. Semen tests showed he belonged to blood group B.

66 ...the killer had sex with Joan before she died. **99**

She had been wearing the clothes she was seen in last – the coat and boots with a turquoise crew neck sweater, bright yellow tank top and brown slacks. She wore a gold chain round her neck and gold loop earrings. That day police and forensics officers sealed off the bloody scene in the back street, and three hours later Joan's battered body was taken away in a hearse.

When the story of her murder broke, David Graham was a 21-year-old reporter at the *Lancashire Evening Post*. Years later he still recalled the day as if it were yesterday. He was sent to the murder scene in Berwick Road after his colleague Jim Potts picked up the details from his morning calls to the police. Mr Graham, who now runs a news agency in Blackpool, told the *Post*, "I remember it was raining, wet, very cold and grey and the sombre weather matched the discovery of the body.

"A constable was standing guard and police had cordoned off the garage itself while scene of crime officers gathered forensic evidence. You couldn't see into the garage and I was told the body had already been taken to the mortuary. Police were doing house-to-house enquiries and I was speaking to the same neighbours." He recalled that, at 10.30pm, police held a press conference and released Joan's name to the media.

The next day, November 25, the headline in the *Lancashire Evening Post* was: "Twilight world of a murder victim." The article read: "Just off Preston's town centre Church Street, the *Post* talked to three men who were about to start a can or two of cider. They knew Mrs Harrison. What they knew is not pleasant."

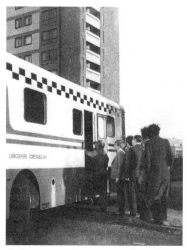

David Graham explained, "There was a reaction from society at the time that she was someone putting herself at risk by the very nature of her lifestyle. We followed up avenues to keep the story going and found ourselves knocking on the doors of semi-derelict homes where people slept rough.

Saliva samples were taken from men who lived and worked in the Avenham area.

"Everywhere we went with connections to Joan was rundown. Some of the homes where people slept rough were covered in cider bottles. We found her circle of friends were drunks and tramps who spent their time around Church Street and out towards Peel Street."

He said the police encountered similar difficulties, having problems tracing Mrs Harrison's movements before her murder because of her lifestyle on the seedier side of Preston life. Many potential interviewees had short memories, blurred by drink and nights roughing it in derelict property. Graham added, "Police had a difficult time when talking to her friends as most didn't know what day it was, let alone what they were doing at 9pm the previous Thursday. It was a mental impossibility to remember any hard facts as many were floating on a sea of alcohol."

One of the prime suspects in the early investigation was Mrs Harrison's landlord and lover David Keighley, but he was later ruled out after offering a cast-iron alibi. But he was not the only one of Joan's former lovers to fall under suspicion. Years later her former boyfriend Wilf Roach told of his time as the prime suspect. He was eventually ruled out following a saliva test.

Joan's ex-lover Wilf Roach.

Thirty years after Joan's murder he told the *Lancashire Evening Post* he had been head over heels in love with her. He found out about her death from the front page of the *Lancashire Evening Post,* brought home by his brother, Bill. His heartbreak turned to horror soon after when he found himself a suspect for her brutal murder. Mr Roach recalled, "Detectives turned up at my flat twice after the murder and spoke to me at work so I felt like the number one suspect for a time. Thirty years on and I would like nothing better than to know whoever did this has got what's coming to them."

He said, "I have always maintained the girl who died was not the same girl I knew and loved. She was a gorgeous girl, warm and loving and a good mum. But she changed after turning to drink and was what I would call a good time girl. I loved her very much and if things had worked out differently I would have asked her to marry me."

He admitted that in the 1970s they were all dabbling in drink and drugs: "I first met her as I had some amphetamines to sell that I didn't want. She would use it to give her the energy to keep her house tidy, but after drink took control she let things slip and missed the mortgage payments and eventually they took the house off her and her kids.

"She moved in with her sister, Margaret Upton, but Joan began selling ornaments and the kids' toys to get money for drink. We split up eventually as she began going out more and more to the pub with her sister's husband, who played music around the town. It made me jealous and we had an argument. I was heartbroken when she finished it. I was quite a lot older than her and I don't think her parents approved. I was a registered drug addict but I decided to give it up after the relationship ended, which meant giving up my lifestyle and friends in those circles. Joan just carried on drinking so I hadn't seen her in a while before she died."

A squad of 80 detectives moved in, with officers drawn from right across Lancashire. Police interviewed almost 100,000 people, and took more than 6,000 statements and saliva samples. The rare blood group of her killer – identified through the bite marks and semen – allowed police to rule out thousands of men who volunteered or who were tracked down to be tested. The discovery that Joan

had sex before she died triggered a probe into the thriving red light district of Avenham, amid theories that the murderer could have been a client or a prostitute-hater.

The man leading the murder inquiry, Detective Superintendent Wilf Brooks, told the *Lancashire Evening Post*, "I am now satisfied that

The murder scene in the back streets of Preston.

there are sexual implications to this murder. The woman had had sex before she died." In fact Joan had had sexual activity with at least five men prior to her death. A special lorry squad was set up to talk to long distance drivers as they rolled in and out of town, also targeting ships' crews and overnight guests at hotels and guest houses.

When Joan's brown purse, believed stolen, was recovered by a member of the public in Avenham Park, the find sparked a massive fingertip search of the park, which including draining the pond to look for clues, to no avail. A hunt for Joan's missing cigarette lighters and jewellery – two gold rings and an engagement ring with three stones set in platinum, and several silver and chrome bracelets – proved a tougher task.

A drunken confession to the murder made by a young man in a pub, known to locals as 'the bar room boaster', was soon ruled out. Even the post mortem examination, carried out straight away on the body, was unable to pinpoint an exact cause or time of death. As the hunt moved into its second week, Det Supt Brooks, then second-in-command of Lancashire CID, admitted it had turned into a "hard slog". He told the *Post* how many members of the murder team had sacrificed home and family life, burning both ends of the CID candle, convinced they would clinch a result on the case.

Meanwhile, hundreds of lines of inquiry were followed and eliminated, with numerous unreliable sightings taken into account. Weeks of routine, methodical checking, re-interviewing, tracing outstanding witnesses were undertaken. Looking for an anonymous tip or a broken alibi, re-visiting pubs and clubs, going over and over statements and working alongside regional crime squads across the country in the hunt for Joan's killer.

Three, four, five weeks passed by, and as time went on Joan's death remained a riddle. Police still had no serious leads. Christmas came and went and still there was no light at the end of the tunnel for investigating officers or any form of closure for Joan's family. Despite a massive probe into Preston's twilight world, sifting through the lives of tramps, winos and down and outs, the dragnet still failed to uncover any solid leads.

One year later, in November 1976, Joan's killer had still not been found. Wilf Brooks continued heading the investigation, despite his promotion to detective chief superintendent and head of Lancashire CID. He was no less determined to crack the case, despite the fact that the number of police assigned to the case had gradually been eroded.

"We are still intent on tracing the killer of Joan Harrison," he vowed. "Information about the incident is still coming in but we would obviously welcome any further help from members of the public."

Then came a remarkable twist to the story that turned a low life murder into national news still discussed to this day.

Three weeks before Joan was killed Wilma McCann, 28, was struck twice with a hammer then stabbed 15 times and her body dumped in a playing field in Leeds. The mother-of-four was the first victim killed by the Yorkshire Ripper. Over the following five years the serial killer struck at least 20 times, butchering 13 women to death and leaving others seriously injured. The crime spree shocked the nation and left women living across the north of England in the grip of terror. In March

1978, the head of the ongoing Ripper Squad, West Yorkshire Constabulary's assistant chief constable George Oldfield, received the first of three letters from a man claiming to be the feared serial killer.

> *Dear Sir,*
> *I'm sorry I can't give my name for obvious reasons. I am the Ripper. I've been dubbed a maniac by the press but not by you, you call me clever and I am.*
>
> *...Up to number eight now you say seven but remember Preston 75, get about a bit you know.*

And he signed off

> *Yours respectfully, Jack the Ripper.*

Soon after, the man calling himself the Ripper put pen to paper again, this time posting the letter to the *Daily Mirror*.

> *Dear Sir,*
> *I have already written to Chief Constable George Oldfield 'a man I respect' concerning the recent Ripper murders. I told him and I am telling you to warn them whores I will strike again and soon when heat cools off.*
> *...Up to number eight now you say seven but remember Preston 75.*
> *...Yours respectfully, Jack the Ripper.*

When the letter arrived at the *Daily Mirror* newsroom, it caused a storm and the editors wanted to publish it. But instead they approached George Oldfield, who was shocked, revealing he had never even received the initial letter. After digging into the police internal mail system, it was uncovered. After protracted negotiations, staff at the *Mirror* agreed to sit on the story for a year to help police investigations. A year passed, and with the letter receiving no publicity, the 'Ripper' decided to make contact again. In March 1979 another letter was received:

> *Dear Officer,*
> *Sorry I haven't written, about a year to be exact, but I haven't been up north for quite a while. I wasn't kidding last time I wrote...*

Frustrated with a lack of publicity, the next contact he made put his voice to his claims for the first time, sending in a tape cassette with a chilling recording. The tape reached George Oldfield on June 17, 1979. In his north east accent, the man claiming to be the Ripper appeared to be playing a strange game of cat and mouse.

The speaker said in a sarcastic tone:

> *"I'm Jack. I see you are still having no luck catching me. I have the greatest respect for you George, but Lord! You are no nearer catching me now than four years ago when I started. No good looking for fingerprints."*

The message ended with laughter. The recording finished with a clip from the song 'Thank You For Being A Friend' by Andrew Gold, and was marked *'From Jack the Ripper'*.

The handwritten letters and audio tape caused a storm. Not only did it swing the spotlight back on to the Joan Harrison case, marking her out as a possible Ripper victim, but it also switched the emphasis of the massive Ripper inquiry over to the north east of England. The tape, heavily edited from ten minutes to two, was played to the media in a bid to trace the speaker.

In a press conference held at a lecture theatre at the police academy at Bishopsgarth, Wakefield, George Oldfield sat alone with a tape player on a table in front of him. When he pressed play, the atmosphere was electric. Oldfield told the assembled press, "I believe we have now got the break we are looking for in our hunt for the so-called Yorkshire Ripper."

The story was huge and the nation was agog.

Yorkshire Police launched a frantic bid to identify him, playing his voice again and again to the enthralled public and pouring vast amounts of their limited resources into tracking him down. As former *Lancashire Evening Post* reporter David Graham recounted, the story of Joan's murder now took on a life of its own:

"When links arose with the Yorkshire Ripper killings, the case began to boil instead of simmer. It gave the investigating team in Preston a chance to pass the buck down the line to West Yorkshire."

West Yorkshire Police were initially convinced by the letters and tape and switched the search to Sunderland. It was to be a costly and tragic mistake that cost the police thousands of man-hours and thousands of pounds, sending detectives up a blind alley and possibly costing three more women their lives.

For 18 months they targeted the area, during which time, Sutcliffe, the real Yorkshire Ripper, was interviewed and eliminated because he did not have a north east accent. Meanwhile, in 1979, the *Lancashire Evening Post* reported that the Ripper was thought to be responsible for Joan's murder.

'Skid Row link-up in Ripper hunt,' read the headline. The story revealed a top-level meeting between Lancashire CID and its counterpart in Yorkshire had led to a sharing of information. It said, "They decided a close similarity existed between the Ripper murders and the killing of mother-of-two Joan Harrison. That attack came less than a month after the first Ripper murders."

Det Supt Donald Griffiths told the *Post*, "There is certainly a marked similarity in the way all the people were attacked and killed. And it could well be the work of the same person."

There was much to link her violent killing with those of the man who called himself the Ripper. He knew about her murder and tests showed Joan's attacker belonged to the rare blood group B secretor, matching the blood grouping of the author of the letters. The blood group is shared by just 6% of the population.

The crime scene echoed a Ripper murder with Joan's boots taken off and placed on top of the rear of her thigh, her body covered with a coat. The bite mark on her breast was similar to that of Ripper victim Josephine Whitaker. Joan's abdominal injuries mirrored those of another Ripper victim, 16-year-old Jayne MacDonald. The use of a hammer as a murder weapon was a Ripper trademark. And Joan's lifestyle and sexual activities mirrored those of most of the Yorkshire killer's victims.

Det Chief Supt Brooks said, "In the light of this new information, what was a distinct possibility that the Ripper killed her has now become a probability." He speculated on why the Ripper would send such a tape and letters: "He could want to get caught or he could be throwing down the gauntlet. There could be all sorts of reasons."

In November 1979, the *Lancashire Evening Post*'s own offices were thrown into the media glare when a man with a Wearside accent rang in to talk about his crimes. The boastful conversation with an *Evening Post* receptionist at the paper's former Fishergate office was recorded and later played to police and the *Post's* then editor Barry Askew. The voice told the receptionist, "I'm Jack," adding, "These fellows the police are not very clever." He claimed he had been to Preston already and said he would strike again soon in the town and in nearby Wigan. The receptionist recognised the voice as being the same as that played on the infamous Ripper tape. The *Evening Post* story headline was 'Ripper voice warns Post: I'll be back'. The story continued, 'Experienced telephonists are convinced it was no hoax. Only hours before they had listened to a police tape of the Ripper's voice. "It was identical," they asserted. It said: "I have a message for George. I will strike again in Preston or Wigan. Tell George he has not got me yet."

The switchboard operator, who was not named in the paper, told the *Post* reporter, "I had been listening to the tape of the Ripper's voice earlier this morning and I am sure the voice was the same. It had the same accent and the man even paused in the same way as the voice on the tape. I felt really shaken up afterwards." Such was the fear inspired by the Yorkshire Ripper and the

> **"** ...the town's street sex trade was all but killed off overnight... **"**

possibility he had struck in Preston, the town's street sex trade was all but killed off overnight and remained so for more than two decades.

Back then, Preston was a busy port and there had been plenty of work for the women in their twenties and thirties who touted for business in the Church Street, Manchester Road and Shepherd Street areas. These areas proved to be a magnet for kerb-crawlers and punters, with sailors and lorry drivers passing through the town regularly

One prostitute, Mary, told the *Evening Post* she worked the same patch as Joan and said she was lucky to be alive. She herself was injured when a "mush" – a man prepared to pay cash for sex – refused to hand over the cash and a scuffle developed, in which she was stabbed. Another said she no longer took men inside strange buildings, saying, "Now I just settle for £10 a time in the back of somebody's car." Another prostitute, Barbara, said, "I always took men back to my flat so I was in screaming distance if necessary. Just after Joan's death we were always talking about the killer. Every night I go to bed, the Ripper tape goes through my mind."

Ripper squad detectives visited Preston repeatedly, even inviting winos and prostitutes to a special briefing on the killer's macabre tape message. But then rumours surfaced that the letters and the tape may well be a hoax. An anonymous tip-off to the Sunderland incident room in 1979 claimed they were fake, and by winter that year speculation was rife, with some police officers voicing their doubts openly.

In turn the speculation cast heavy doubts over any links between Joan's murder and the Ripper. And several factors, predominantly that Joan was not stabbed and the killer had sex with her before the attack, added to the argument.

Then on January 5, 1981, the *Post* reported that the Yorkshire Ripper had finally been caught by the police the day before.

'Ripper: Man held' screamed the headline. The following day, with the Ripper denying Joan's murder, the *Evening Post* headline was 'Preston killer still on run', with Det Chf Insp Brookes telling the *Post* there was always a possibility the letters and tape were a hoax. He added, "I want to stress that our inquiries into the death of Joan Harrison will continue elsewhere."

Then the Yorkshire Ripper, named as 35-year-old lorry driver Peter Sutcliffe from Bradford, appeared in court in connection with a string of murders across Yorkshire and Greater Manchester. He was sentenced to life imprisonment admitting carrying out 13 killings, but crucially, not that of Joan Harrison. Under interrogation, he told police they could not connect him to the crime. Added to the fact that his blood group was B, not B secretor, it looked increasingly unlikely he was her killer.

> **" [The Yorkshire Ripper] told police they could not connect him to the crime. "**

Some facts were still puzzling, however. When Sutcliffe was eventually detained, he had a gap in his teeth which could have matched the marks on Mrs Harrison's body. The possibility that Joan was hit in the head with a ball hammer, a weapon used by Sutcliffe, aroused suspicion, as did the fact her shoes were taken off and placed on her legs, again a trait of Sutcliffe's murders. The scene of Joan's murder also had chilling similarities to the northern back streets trawled by Sutcliffe in his hunt for victims. But at his trial at London's Old Bailey, attempts were made to put any links between the crimes to bed.

The judge told the court, "The scent was falsified by a cynical, almost inhuman hoaxer – I refer to the tape and letters. I express the hope that one day he may be exposed." After the trial the investigations into both Joan Harrison's murder and the Ripper hoaxer, dubbed 'Wearside Jack', went quiet.

At the end of 1981 the Wearside Jack inquiry was wound down. Embarrassed by the costly red herring, the police left the trail of Wearside Jack to go stale, brushing aside the possibility that he could have been Joan's real killer. Although both cases remained open, police resources were diverted elsewhere. So the scent went cold, leaving the field open for speculation and investigation by several journalists determined to get to the bottom of the mystery. One such journalist was Patrick Lavelle, an investigative journalist who for many years maintained Peter Sutcliffe was Joan Harrison's killer. He has now changed his mind.

In one of his three books on the subject, *The Shadow of the Ripper*, and during television documentaries, he claimed the Ripper carried out the killing in the company of another man – the same man who sent hoax letters and a tape to police. With his past theories rejected by police, Mr Lavelle said the links between the Ripper killings and Joan Harrison's death were more than coincidence. In his book, he calls for Sutcliffe to be questioned about her death. He told the *Evening Post* in 2003 that Sutcliffe would never admit to killing Joan because of his loyalty to a "friend" present at the time.

But on the 30th anniversary of the day Joan's body was discovered, he was to tell the *Lancashire Evening Post*, "The murder has been a running story and what I thought originally does not really stand now because of new evidence. I hope that this new evidence and scientific developments will see the case eventually solved.

"I now believe Wearside Jack, who sent letters and a tape to police claiming to be the Yorkshire Ripper, was just a hoaxer who got information from national newspapers and used phraseology of the Ripper to write his letters." Mr Lavelle was not the only author to have claimed to have unearthed the truth behind the Preston murder. Another man, Irish author Noel O'Gara claimed to be able to prove that although Sutcliffe carried out some of the killings, a second, 'real Ripper' was on the loose and responsible for killing Joan.

Mr O'Gara claimed, "Both Leeds prostitute Wilma McCann and Mrs Harrison had been violently murdered and robbed of their jewellery. Both had been sexually assaulted and both had their boots removed and coats draped over their dead bodies."

In March 1977, Scots girl Irene Richardson was also found murdered in Leeds with the same bite mark in her left breast. By the time Sutcliffe was arrested in 1980, building society clerk Josephine Whittaker had also been killed and had the same bite mark. According to O'Gara, although Sutcliffe had a gap in his front teeth, the imprint did not match those on the murdered women. His blood group also differed from that found in the saliva and he was cleared of the Harrison murder. But, Mr O'Gara disputes, if the original murder victims bore identical teeth marks and saliva traces to those on Joan's body, they must have been committed by the same person.

Mr O'Gara said, "If Sutcliffe had not killed Mrs Harrison, he could not and did not kill the prostitutes. It was well known that there was a copy-cat killer at the time and I believe Sutcliffe was this copy-cat killer."

> **❝ I believe Sutcliffe was this copy-cat killer. ❞**

When Sutcliffe was caught, Sir Lawrence Byford, an inspector of constabulary, concluded the West Yorkshire Police incident room was "sadly inefficient" which lead to a failure to pinpoint the Bradford man as a prime suspect. His report – written in 1982, but only coming to light in 2006 through the Freedom of Information Act – led to a complete overhaul of the way murders are investigated, and led to the introduction of nationwide computer database of all murders committed in the UK.

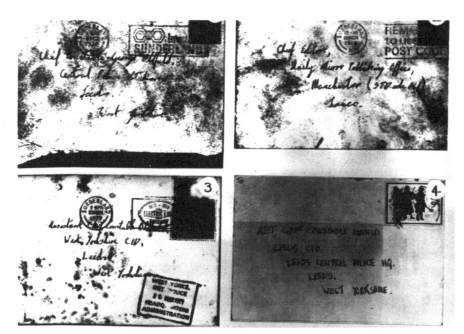

Hoax letters from Wearside Jack.

The report also revealed a new twist. A chilling painting by Yorkshire Ripper, Peter Sutcliffe, reopened the decades long debate…did he kill Joan? The picture, created behind bars by the serial killer, bears an eerie similarity to one of Preston's main streets and the cafe in the foreground is called Joan's. The Byford report said Sutcliffe probably did commit more attacks than the 13 killings and seven attempted murders he admitted to, pointing to an "unexplained lull" in his activities between 1969 and 1975. It said a number of assaults on women between 1969 and 1980 "clearly fall" into the pattern of Sutcliffe's method of working. And this artwork painted by the killer shows an unnamed street with a distinctly 1970s feel, which is similar to the Preston that Joan would have known.

Detectives in Preston say their colleagues investigating the case saw the findings of the report at the time. Det Insp Chris Wilde of Preston CID, who had not seen the painting, told the *Evening Post*, "Whether a picture that looked a bit like Preston would be damning evidence, I don't know.

"It does seem a bit weird that there is a cafe called Joan's. But it might just be his sick twisted mind and he would do something like that just to get us all doing what we are doing now. I can say with some degree of certainty that Peter Sutcliffe was suspected of killing Joan Harrison back in the 1970s. He has been questioned about it but has always denied it." Twenty years after Joan's death, police said the police file was still open. Det Chief Insp Bill Hacking, head of Lancashire CID in November 1995, told the *Post*, "It was 20 years ago, but it is still a life that has been lost and the file remains open."

He added the Yorkshire Ripper connection was now closed down, saying police were "as satisfied as we could be that he was not responsible."

John Humble, known as Wearside Jack.

It was to be almost 25 years after Sutcliffe went to prison for life that Wearside Jack would hit the front pages again. A cold case review by West Yorkshire police's new homicide and enquiry team using new DNA and forensic technology to examine letters and envelopes, led detectives to a two-bedroom terraced house in Flodden Road, Sunderland, and an alcoholic former hospital porter and security guard, John Humble.

In October 2005 the 49-year-old unemployed divorcee, blood type B secretor, was arrested on suspicion of attempting to pervert the course of justice by posing as the Yorkshire Ripper. Rumours immediately spread that he would be questioned

❝ John Humble admitted he was Wearside Jack. ❞

about Joan's murder, but they fell flat when police just charged him with perverting the course of justice. John Humble admitted he was Wearside Jack.

In March 2006 he appeared in Leeds Crown Court in front of packed press and public galleries, pleading not guilty to four counts of perverting the course of justice. He claimed he had retracted his hoax claims but was found guilty and jailed.

A quarter of a decade later, the mystery was solved, but Joan's killer remains at large. To some she was a prostitute, to others simply a good-time girl who had a lot of friends. But she was a young woman who still had a chance of bringing her life back on track, had it not been stolen away from her on that cold winter day. Instead, as the enigma of Joan's terrible death continues to plague her family, her killer could still be walking these very streets.

CHAPTER TWO

A mother's wrath

Alan Livesey, Bamber Bridge, February 22, 1979

Gently, a cross of pink and white roses and carnations was laid down on the newly turned earth. Six feet under the cold soil, finally at rest, lay the body of a young boy. And placed carefully on top of the grave was a note: "In loving memory of Alan. From Mum, Dad, Janet, Derek and Frank." A moving tribute to a life tragically cut short, from a family mourning the loss of a teenager snatched from them in the cruellest of ways.

But behind the emotional scenes on that dark day, not all was what it seemed. While most of the family members struggled to cope with their grief and shock, one of them was missing from the teenager's graveside after exposing a terrible secret. It was an admission that had left a family torn apart and a community reeling with shock and disgust. Nobody could quite believe the chain of events.

Pink and white roses and carnations laid at the graveside.

Young Alan Livesey – just 14 – had been murdered. But by whose hand?

The year was 1979. While for some the seventies was a decade of freedom and expression, for young Alan Livesey they were dark days growing up within the confines of a difficult, working class family.

Home for Alan, the youngest of three children, was a red-bricked council house at The Crescent, in the industrial town of Bamber Bridge near Preston. He lived with his parents, Margaret and Bob. His sister Janet had recently married and left home; his brother Derek was in the army and based in Germany.

A pupil at nearby Walton-le-Dale High School, slightly-built Alan was a typical teenager, rebelling against the strictures of his parents and teachers, and determined to find his own way in the world.

Like many youngsters trapped in similar situations, Alan would escape the endless arguments and difficulties of his strained home life by staying out of the house with friends. He and best friend, Andrew Matthews, would share their frustrations and dreams with each other, building a secret den with a crumpled tent, a polythene sheet and a strip of carpet in a hawthorn thicket near their homes to hide in. Alan was also a member of the Walton-le-Dale youth centre, a popular hangout for young boys.

But the fair-haired teenager's first love was the army. Hoping to follow his elder brother Derek's escape route as a serving soldier, he was an enthusiastic member of the Lancashire Army Cadet Force, which was then attached to the Queen's Lancashire Regiment.

Along with best pal Andrew, he attended meetings twice a week, on Mondays and Wednesdays, as well as taking part in events on occasional weekends. Proudly, the pair would head off together wearing the uniforms they looked after so carefully. But, as Andrew later told, the cadet force was as much an escape as a fulfilment of a dream. Alan was not just tired of his difficult home life; he was also living in mortal terror of his hard-drinking mother. Andrew remembered calling at Alan's house several times, only to find him crying in an armchair:

"He was really frightened of his mum. He regularly got thumped two or three times a week. He was keen on the cadets but I think he went sometimes just to get out of the house."

In fact drink was the constant companion of Margaret Livesey. After growing up in the licensed trade, she turned to the bottle in her married life and was to have a glass in her hand when she calmly received the news, "Your son is dead."

The 43-year-old brunette had a reputation for the amount she could knock back, her husband Bob saying later, "She could take a lot. But I never once put her to bed drunk. I supposed she had a drink problem, yes, but not a bad one. It was never a craving for her, nothing as bad as that. She just used to like her drink."

Neighbours agreed, including friend Marion Walker: "It's true, she liked a drink but I must say I had never seen her drunk. I didn't even know she drank at home."

On February 22, Margaret had been out to a sing-along evening at her local pub, while her husband worked the night shift at Leyland Vehicles. She had also been drinking cider at home, where she had a regular order for two flagons a day from the local off licence, before leaving to meet Marion at the Queen's Hotel in Bamber Bridge.

Margaret was driven home by a friend, but moments later, she was out in the cold night air again, knocking on a neighbour's door. The Matthews family was sitting watching television with another neighbour, Mrs Sarah Rogers, and the late night visit was a surprise. But they offered her a drink and she sat on the arm of a chair as they chatted. "Nip down and see if your Andrew is at our house with Alan," said Margaret to the Matthews' eldest son, Leslie.

The 17-year-old strolled down to the house. At first he could get no answer. The television was turned up loud. So he returned home and Margaret gave him a key to get in. He opened the front door, walked inside and a strong smell of gas immediately hit him as he entered the living room.

The Livesey home in Bamber Bridge.

The gruesome discovery he made there was to haunt him for the rest of his life. Alan was lying face down on the rug in front of the fire. His hands were bound behind him with his yellow and blue school tie. Panicking, Leslie ran to him.

Mrs Matthews said later, "Les came running back, he was covered in blood. He just walked into the living room and put his head in his hands. We asked him what was up. He just said 'I don't know how to tell you. Alan's dead'. Later after the police had come, Les told us he had rolled Alan over and he had groaned. He had tried the kiss of life but it was no good. There was blood everywhere."

Alan had been murdered in a horrific attack – an attack so frenzied it left investigators sickened to the stomach. He had been stabbed up to ten times in the neck and body, several of the knife blows so violent they penetrated his heart, lungs, spine and jaw. Two of the knife blows passed through his neck from front to back. Alan's small body was bound up and left in a pool of blood on the floor. In a strange twist he was wearing his full cadet combat uniform, even though it was not the usual night of a meeting. The home's gas tap had been turned full on. Police swooped on the scene of the murder and during the long, traumatic night that followed, the Liveseys and the Matthews sat together in shock, drinking tea and talking. Only once that night did Alan's mum give way to her emotions and burst into tears. The rest of the time she remained composed, apparently in shock, sleeping for a while in an armchair by the window.

The next day the story broke and Preston reacted with horror. 'Bizarre killing of boy soldier, 14,' splashed across the *Lancashire Evening Post*, reporting that Alan's parents were under sedation as their house was sealed off and searched. It reported, "The teenager had been left alone playing in the lounge with his Scalextric racing set. It is understood he was wearing purple corduroy trousers and shirt when his mother went out. But when Alan's body was discovered two hours later he was wearing full cadet combat clothes and boots, and had his hands tied behind his back"

Leslie Matthews, 17, who found the body.

A neighbour told the paper they had heard 'play-fighting' between Alan and one other person before 10pm. "Suddenly it went quiet," she said. "It was quite normal to hear him and other lads messing about."

Police called a press conference and appealed for information. Detective Superintendent Ian Hunter, deputy head of Lancashire CID, was put in charge of the investigation. "If anyone can help regarding this boy's movements last night I appeal to them to come forward. He may have been seen out wearing his army gear, we just don't know. He may have left the house. As far as we can determine the house was not forcibly entered."

He added that when Alan's mother left to go to the pub that evening Alan had been wearing purple trousers and a white T-shirt with the words "I'm with stupid" written on the front. "We don't know at this stage why he was wearing the army gear because it was not his usual cadet night."

An army spokesman confirmed the cadets were not allowed to wear their uniforms on other occasions without special permission from Commanding Officer, Captain Jim Eskdale.

A team of 50 officers was put to task, conducting door-to-door enquiries. Police with tracker dogs were also brought to the area to search for evidence. Gardens and drains were searched. A mobile police station was set up in Bamber Bridge and posters of Alan were issued. Meanwhile, local undertaker BJ Watson removed the body from the lounge floor, wrapped in a plastic sheet. Home Office Pathologist, Dr Gordon Benstead, then embarked on the grim task of carrying out a post mortem examination on Alan's mutilated body.

> **❝ I cannot think of any reason anyone would want to do this. ❞**

Alan's brother Derek, 19, was told about the murder during a skiing holiday. He returned from his base in Germany to be by his family's side. Bowed with grief, he could not understand why this tragedy had happened. "I cannot think of any reason anyone would want to do this. Alan was very well liked. He was keen on the army, he was always asking me what the army was like."

The community of Bamber Bridge mourned. Few could believe the full horrific picture emerging from the stabbing of the 14-year-old. Sympathy flowed for Alan's parents, made more poignant when their picture appeared in the *Lancashire Evening Post* a few days later. Both agreed to be interviewed by journalists in the hope of flushing out the killer. Alan's father, Bob, told the paper, as his wife sat silently by his side, "It is a complete mystery to us. We think someone, somewhere, knows something – we can't think of anyone who would do such a horrible thing."

At Alan's school, the headteacher John Cox told 1,000 pupils, "We have a serious criminal somewhere in the district. Tell the police all you know, this is a terrible business."

Alan's closest friend Andrew, 15, decided he couldn't face the cadet meetings anymore without his friend and resigned from the unit, though he was allowed to keep his uniform. But his commanding officer told journalists he was too scared to walk the streets in it any more.

Two days after the murder, police were still baffled.

Unable to pinpoint a firm suspect, they investigated theories that Alan had died in a war game that had gone wrong, which were rubbished by his commanding officer. Capt Eskdale, of Farington, Leyland, told the *Evening Post*, "He wasn't trained in self defence of any kind. Alan was mad keen to join up. But we have never practised anything with hand weapons like knives, that sort of thing was completely alien to him and his training." Eskdale told how Alan would have made a fine soldier, probably a good corporal or sergeant, adding, "He lived for the army, he was like a kid waiting for his birthday. When he joined up 12 months ago he was a bit quieter than most of the lads, but once he settled in, he showed he was going to be a model cadet."

But a picture had begun to be painted of young Alan's troubled life. It emerged he had twice been in trouble with the police and was awaiting a court appearance for taking a car and crashing it. His behaviour had seen his already strained relationship with his parents, particularly his mum, sink to a new low. Neighbours muttered about the many rows in the household and speculation about who killed the boy was rife.

Then, five days after Alan's tragic death, there was a twist nobody had seen coming. During extensive interviews with police, Margaret Livesey dramatically confessed to murdering her son.

In a signed statement to police, she admitted, "I stabbed him again and again in the throat and all the time I was thinking 'you little bad sod'."

" ...all the time I was thinking 'you little bad sod'. "

She was immediately charged by police, appearing weeping at Leyland magistrates' court wearing a black hooded sweater with the hood down before being remanded in custody. A pathetic figure, she appeared flanked by two policewomen as her husband Bob watched silently at the back of the court. The community was buffeted by shock at the revelation. How could a mother possibly murder her child so savagely in cold blood? Disbelieving, her husband stood by her side, convinced of her innocence.

But it later emerged that, following her confession, she had put her arms around son Derek, saying, "I'm sorry Derek, I am sorry son, please forgive me, I don't know what made me do it."

Then having put her arm round her husband, she said, "I am sorry Bob, you know what he was like, he just drove me to it," to which Mr Livesey replied, "Why didn't you tell me? We've talked about it for hours." She replied, "I couldn't, I just couldn't." He then said, "You didn't have to do this."

She replied, "I just snapped, I'm sorry."

With the start of March, came the saddest of days. Flanked by his remaining son, daughter and son-in-law, Bob Livesey laid his youngest child to rest while his wife languished behind bars, awaiting a court appearance the very next day.

Scores of mourners turned out to pay their last respects to the teenager at the special service at St Aidan's Church in Bamber Bridge, and at the graveside in the grounds of St Saviour's Church. Dozens more silently lined the roadside as the funeral cortege made its way slowly along the town's main street.

Officers from Alan's army cadet detachment carried the coffin, draped with the unit's standard, to the graveside. Among the mourners were Alan's classmates and his headmaster who read a lesson to the large congregation. The church was adorned with flowers from army cadet units throughout central Lancashire, as well as from pals from two youth clubs and wreaths from neighbours and school friends.

Rev Christopher Kingston told the mourners, "This is not the occasion for macabre speculation. It is not our duty at this service to dwell upon the circumstances of his death. In our prayers we will ask God for comfort for Alan's family." Bob, Derek and Janet were so overcome with grief they had to be helped from Alan's graveside. After three days on remand in prison, Margaret Livesley had withdrawn her confession; claiming the words had been put into her mouth by police and that they had bullied her. She would plead not guilty to killing her son and face trial for murder.

So in June 1979 a jury was convened at Preston High Court and the court proceedings began. The courtroom drama attracted long queues of people for the public gallery. But it would take two trials in Preston's austere court number two, lasting a total of 13 days, for justice to be done.

On the eighth working day of the trial, when the jury had been considering their verdict for some two days, a problem emerged. Dramatically the jury was discharged after one member had to be excused because of a seriously ill relative. But the defence team were not prepared to continue with just 11 jurors. A new jury had to be selected and on July 19 a fresh trial began, the prosecution and defence arguments played out again in full in front of the rapt court.

The intensive media coverage of both trials was lapped up by the local community, enthralled by the horrific murder as it played out in detail. 'Army boy "stabbed to death in rage"' was the headline of the *Lancashire Evening Post* on July 2 as the first trial began. Margaret Livesey was accused of killing her youngest son after a violent row, before wrapping a football sock around his neck to hide the blood and then tying his hands behind his back.

Prosecuting counsel Miss Joyanne Bracewell told the court, "She stabbed him to death with a kitchen knife which she had previously left in the living room after peeling potatoes. Having stabbed him to the chest, he fell to the ground so she wrapped a football sock round his neck and then stabbed him through the sock, either to stop blood spurting out or so she would not see the blood. She then tied his hands to make it look like an outsider had done it."

The exact words of Margaret's confession were repeated. In an interview with police she had said, "He fell to the floor. I stabbed him again and again. I turned him over. I didn't want to have to look at him. It was the blood. Forgive me Alan, I didn't mean to do it, son." The court heard Margaret admit having a row with Alan over his general misbehaviour and because she suspected him of shoplifting. The statement went on, "I called him a liar, a cheat and a thief and that he was a stranger to the truth. He got up. I slapped him across the face. I then saw a little kitchen knife and picked it up.

"I remember stabbing him a number of times. He fell to the floor and I stabbed him again in the throat. I was thinking 'You little bad sod' all the time and I had completely lost control of myself. I just couldn't look at him when I saw the blood, so I turned him over. The next thing I remember was outside in the street." The confession continued: "Subconsciously I wanted to make it look like someone else had done it. I just couldn't believe that I had done it."

She then said she asked the son of a neighbour to go down to the house: "I remember him saying when he came back that Alan was dead and I said I would go with him. I was hoping at that time that he wasn't dead and everything would be all right."

When charged with murder she apologised for her actions, "I only wish to say I'm sorry for what I did. I didn't mean it to happen. I wouldn't for the world have harmed my son intentionally.

❝ ...I was under pressure at the time and my mind must have snapped. ❞

I was under pressure at the time and my mind must have snapped."

A neighbour had heard voices during the row which she identified as Mrs Livesey and Alan. The boy had screamed "help me", with the word "me" tailing away. After that everything had gone quiet. The defence argued that Margaret's confession had been obtained through coercion and actually she had gone straight to the Matthews' house after being dropped off from the pub. Margaret, protesting her innocence, later claimed she was forced into the confession by police. She told the court the first she heard of her son's death was when Leslie returned with the news.

As the court drama played out, the public gallery was packed with queues forming every day. The headlines continued, "Stabbed army cadet an unwanted child."

Alan Livesey.

Margaret, it was alleged, had not just confessed to the murder; she had shown regular signs of disliking her youngest son. Neighbours claimed the teenager was regularly ignored, told to "go away" or just given a "clip round the ear". Mrs Susan Warren, whose home adjoined the Livesey house, told the court Margaret had even admitted that "she didn't even want Alan... meaning she hadn't wanted to conceive him."

Next door neighbours Mrs Warren and Christine Norris both told murder trial judge Mr Justice Talbot that Margaret had frequently turned her back on the boy when he tried to talk to her.

Mrs Warren told jurors, "Sometimes she behaved terribly to him. She ignored him, couldn't be bothered with him. If he asked her a question she would tell him to go away, she couldn't be bothered to answer him. I saw her do that a couple of times. Alan just walked away, disappointed. I don't think there was a relationship between Alan and his mother really."

She said she regularly heard rows between the woman and her son and didn't think anything of a further row on the night of the murder, between 10.30pm and 11pm. She added, "I didn't give it a thought."

Mrs Norris, whose house was on the other side of the Livesey house but separated by a garden, said, "Mrs Livesey hadn't much time for Alan. She was impatient with him, indifferent with him, didn't spend much time with him." She explained Margaret had little time for him when he got in trouble with the police, giving him several clips round the ear.

Describing the Liveseys as a "rough" family, she said that on the night of the murder she heard a row and sat straight up in bed with shock, but then the noise went away.

But both neighbours admitted withholding certain information from police when first interviewed.

Mrs Warren said, "I didn't want to get involved. I didn't want to come here."

Defence barrister John Hugill later accused neighbour and witness Mrs Matthews, "You have decided Mrs Livesey is guilty and you and all the other neighbours in the area are altering your evidence and not telling the truth."

The murder weapon.

Were they telling the truth now?

The police evidence appeared flawless. Det Insp Harry Mariner told how Margaret confessed under questioning. After starting out confident and in high spirits, her mood soon changed: "That attitude hardened when we told her there were discrepancies in her statement. She became very wary, she looked very tense, she was sitting on the edge of the chair. Then after that she started to put her head in her hands and started to use tissues as if she was crying."

At first, he said, Margaret had asked, "Do you really think that I could murder my own son? I wouldn't harm a hair on his bloody head, I wouldn't and everybody knows that." She accused the police of allowing the real murderer to go free. But then her story completely changed and she made her

" I wouldn't harm a hair on his bloody head, I wouldn't and everybody knows that. "

dramatic confession, saying, "Well you know what I did then. I stabbed him and stabbed him."

Det Insp Mariner said, "She wept openly, it was as if a weight had been lifted from her shoulders." He said, after she made a full statement, she said, "What will Bob say?" and "What will people think of me?"

With the court in thrall, heavily bloodstained clothes were held up to show the jury the stab wounds that killed Alan. Home Office pathologist John Benstead described in detail the extent of the young boy's appalling injuries, including the ten separate stab wounds. He told the court the boy died of blood loss and shock following his injuries. "All would have required considerable force," he added.

Forensic scientist Dr Michael Harris showed the jury Alan's bloodstained cadet uniform, along with items of clothing belonging to his mother, said to have been worn by her on the night of her son's death. All had traces of blood on them.

He held up Alan's fawn T-shirt, so badly stained the true colour could only be seen on parts of the sleeves. It had several small holes in the front. The rest of Alan's uniform was also displayed, including a combat sweater which was bloody and torn, a khaki shirt which was stained and punctured and the boy's camouflage pants and studded boots which bore marks of blood. Margaret's black raincoat had bloodstains on the front and right arm. But Dr Harris explained the stains could have been made when she cradled her son. But he said the small amount of blood on the coat was "surprising", adding, "I am quite certain the back of his head was bathed in a pool of blood."

The scene of the crime was explained in detail – blood had been found on the front door lock, on a key and key ring, and in the lining of Margaret's handbag. But a wooden-handled vegetable knife recovered from the cutlery drawer and considered to be the murder weapon had no traces of blood at all. However, a stained towel and a piece of emery paper found near the body also had evidence of human blood on them. Elements of doubt were introduced to the jury and the atmosphere in the packed court was tense. With a full press bench, the court heard about a short period of time Margaret could not account for her whereabouts which could hold the key to the murder.

"Twelve missing minutes on night of death," screamed the *Lancashire Evening Post* headline.

The prosecution claimed the missing minutes occurred when Margaret killed her son. Miss Bracewell said she arrived at her home in The Crescent before 11pm on "this dreadful night". But she didn't arrive at her neighbour's house until some 10 or 12 minutes later.

"It cannot be explained in her evidence, but it can be explained in the argument and the killing of this young boy. The background of this case is of a mother deeply disappointed in the conduct of her son, a son who is causing her so much anguish that she is worried about going out for fear of what he will get up to. She had been crying earlier that evening.

"Was this not all building up on her slowly but surely into a state of desperation?"

But John Hugill, defending, was adamant that Margaret would have had no more than 60 seconds to commit the crime, flee the scene and stage an elaborate cover up. He said the case was a jigsaw puzzle, telling the jury, "If you can't fit every single piece then there is something wrong." He added, "I can and I will put forward a very powerful case that she is innocent."

The defence put forward a twist to the tale, suggesting an alternative scenario for Alan's death.

"Was Alan killed in a torture game?" asked the *Lancashire Evening Post*, as Mr Hugill explained the boy could have died in a bizarre game copying torture and murder in Ulster. A bloodstained newspaper bearing two stories about the activities of a terrorist knife gang in Northern Ireland was found near the body, it was revealed. But, he added, "It may be no more than an extraordinary coincidence."

The two articles dealt with a gang of torturers who cut their victims about the head and neck – Alan was also cut and stabbed in these areas.

He also inferred that Margaret's original confession statement could be inaccurate, "The record of the police in this case with regard to statements isn't particularly happy. The real art of interrogation is that you get someone of a certain calibre and subject them to a certain pressure, then you get them to believe what you put to them," he added, claiming the argument that Margaret was innocent was "flawless".

Leslie Matthews, who found Alan's body, was put on the stand and as he gave his evidence, Margaret wept. The 17-year-old told the High Court, "I tried to give him the kiss of life but blood just gurgled out of his throat. I tried to listen to see if he was breathing, I got blood on my hands and my face."

He said Alan had been on the floor with his hands tied when he arrived at the house and there was a strong smell of gas. "I went over and said, 'Are you alright Alan?' I thought he was mucking about, tied up like that. There was no answer so I turned him over. He made a funny groaning noise and his chest was wet. I took a sock away from his neck and saw a lot of cuts. I thought he was still alive so I tried to give him the kiss of life."

When he failed to resuscitate Alan, he ran back home to tell Margaret, who was drinking and chatting with his parents. Matthews said, "She knelt down and cradled Alan's head in her hands. She said she didn't want him to die with his eyes open."

The trial almost complete, Judge Talbot summed up the case telling jurors to bear in mind times given by witnesses, evidence from the neighbours and Margaret's own statement. They went away to deliberate. After some four and three quarter hours on day six of the trial, they returned with a unanimous verdict.

Guilty.

Murderer Margaret Livesey.

As the verdict was read out in court, there were gasps from the public gallery. Margaret stumbled in the dock as she tried to sit down after the decision. Helped to her feet by two women prison officers, she gave a nervous smile to Mr Justice Talbot. He told he had no alternative but to jail her for life. It seemed the mother who said she didn't do it, would spend at least a decade behind bars. Her solicitor confirmed there would be no appeal. She was initially sent to Holloway women's prison in London.

Despite the finding of the court and the words of his wife, Bob pledged to wait for Margaret until she was released, saying, "I am standing by her as I always have. I will wait however long it takes."

Within hours of her sentencing, whispers of a sensational miscarriage of justice became apparent. Anonymous letters were circulated to the news organisations, an MP and local clergy. Rumours were rife in Bamber Bridge.

By September 1980, Margaret had been in prison for more than a year and was still maintaining her innocence. But leave for an appeal was refused by the judge. Three years later, in October 1983, the BBC's *Rough Justice* programme launched its own investigation, throwing up information, which it claimed proved Margaret's innocence.

The half hour documentary, called "*The case of the tortured teenager*," claimed that Alan was slowly tortured to death and not killed by his jailed mother. It produced new witnesses and claimed Margaret's conviction was unsound, as she did not have the time to stab her son; that vital information was withheld from the defence; that witnesses changed their version of events; and that the original confession was made under pressure. It also suggested the young boy's death had homosexual overtones. The programme was given little credence by local police.

One new witness, Peter Nightingale of School Street, Bamber Bridge, told the BBC he had seen a mystery blond man, around around 5ft 10ins tall, in an anorak near the house on the night of the murder. Forensic expert professor James Cameron also appeared and said the attack was slow, rather than frenzied.

After the show was aired, *Rough Justice* producer Peter Hill categorically told the *Post*, "This lady could not have done this murder." But the police were not taking the criticism lying down. A spokesman for Lancashire Police said, "This force does not want to substitute trial by TV for trial by judge and jury."

" This lady could not have done this murder. "

Later, criticism was also levelled at the BBC team by some of those who featured in the film and reconstruction, who claimed their words and interviews were skewed. But on November 26, 1983, legal pressure group JUSTICE submitted a detailed memo to the Home Office explaining their disquiet about the conviction. By mid-December, West Yorkshire Police was brought in to re-investigate the case "as an absolute priority".

Lead by Assistant Chief Constable John Bennion, the six-month long probe brought little new information to the table despite statements taken from 78 witnesses. When a mystery letter arrived at the *Evening Post* he appealed for the writer to come forward. The writer had sent reams of correspondence over the year alleging Margaret's innocence but never left his name. He never came forward.

By 1984, hopes of an appeal for Margaret were dashed due to a lack of new evidence and the Home Office revealed there were no new grounds for appeal. But those convinced of Margaret's innocence did not give up. In 1985, following another JUSTICE dossier to the Home Office and a second *Rough Justice* programme on the case, the Secretary of State Douglas Hurd finally referred the whole case to the Court of Appeal. The announcement brought a jubilant response from her supporters and JUSTICE as well as being a personal triumph for Preston's then MP Stan Thorne, who had campaigned for her freedom for several years.

It was another full year before Margaret, now in Styal Prison in Cheshire, where she was studying for an Open University degree in social studies, heard her fate following the conclusion of the Court of Appeal case. In December 1986, there came a damning verdict from the second highest court in the land. The judgement in R v. Margaret Livesey read, "We have carefully considered all these matters and we are not of the view that this conviction was in any way unsafe or unsatisfactory. The more information that was adduced before us, the more we became convinced that the verdict of the jury was correct. This appeal is dismissed."

Margaret, by then 51, remained a convicted killer. The following year she was again under the spotlight, this time thanks to a campaigning author who threw the case open to public scrutiny. Bob Woffinden devoted a chapter of his book *Miscarriages of Justice* to the fate of the Bamber Bridge mum, focusing on the way the Court of Appeal dealt with the case.

Then in October 1989, ten years after she was convicted of murdering her young son, Margaret Livesey was released from jail on life parole, still claiming her innocence, saying, "It's fantastic to be free." She told the *Lancashire Evening Post* bitterly, "I have served ten long years for something I didn't do and there are still definitely a lot of things that need answering."

> **❝ I have served ten long years for something I didn't do... ❞**

Her husband Bob, who had now found love elsewhere and started a new life in Clayton Brook, seemed astonished at the news, telling the *Post*, "It has nothing to do with me now."

She may have gained her freedom, but life as Margaret had known it was over. It had seemed the very worst of crimes. Could a mother possibly murder her child in cold blood simply because he was naughty?

A jury found that she could.

Or was Margaret Livesey's conviction for the murder of her son Alan a devastating miscarriage of justice that had allowed the real killer to walk free? Decades after his death there are still more questions than answers, but one thing is clear. Whatever happened, Alan Livesey had his young life cruelly snatched away, something Bamber Bridge residents will never forget.

CHAPTER THREE

The mystery of the handless corpse

Marty Johnstone, Carnforth, October 7, 1979

The water lay still, freezing and inky black, the surface reflecting the gloomy October sky above. Twenty-five feet below, two divers glided silently along the edge of the flooded Eccleston Delph quarry, their movements causing small ripples on the surface as they slowly made their way round the edge in the eerie half light. For keen amateur sub-aqua enthusiasts, mechanic Jeff Ashcroft, 22, and his pal, lorry driver Ian Reading, 34, this was an enjoyable way to spend a Sunday morning, a break away from the daily routine. A mini adventure as they looked out for interesting objects hidden in the cavernous and chilly depths of the beauty spot at Heskin, near Chorley.

The quarry on Halfpenny Lane was popular with dog walkers and courting couples and was sometimes used by the police for diver training. But October 14, 1979 was a quiet, cool, day and Jeff and Ian had no idea of the horrors that were about to unfold.

What they found in the waters was to be beyond their wildest nightmares and triggered an unprecedented police investigation which would eventually touch all four corners of the globe. Their discovery would not only rip apart one of the biggest and most complex criminal organisations in the world, but it would also weed out the evil masterminds who had previously thought themselves untouchable.

It was Ian who saw it first. Just visible through the murky waters of the quarry, he spotted what looked like a tailor's dummy perched grotesquely on a sliver of rock. Signalling to Jeff, Ian slowly swam closer and they prodded the object curiously, peering through their divers masks. Then the reality of what they had found hit them and panicking, both men spluttered to the surface, gasping for breath. Far down below in a terrible watery grave, the two friends had discovered a butchered and hideously scarred body. The find was to spark an

> **❝ ...the two friends had discovered a butchered and hideously scarred body. ❞**

Halfpenny Lane, and the road leading to Eccleston Delph.

unbelievable tale about nine men and women prepared to kill even loved ones to protect a multi-million pound drugs empire. The divers, both from Ashton-in-Makerfield, near Wigan, and members of the Newton-le-Willows scuba club, raised the alarm and a huge police operation swung into action.

Some of Lancashire's top officers were summoned to the scene 50 yards along Halfpenny Lane, including Lancashire CID chief detective, Chief Supt Wilf Brookes, and Assistant Chief Constable Keith Brown. Chorley's Chief Supt Ian Hunter and Superintendent Phil Cafferty of the No. 2 District Task Force based in Penwortham were also called into action. PC Arthur Marshall was a police diver, one of around 100 police officers assigned to the taskforce. He was tasked with heading down into the waters to retrieve the gruesome find. He went out in a dinghy and over the side. As he swam down into the chilling darkness, local anglers continued to fish at the quarry unaware of the drama unfolding beneath them.

The spot had been used in the past for the illegal dumping of cars, and PC Marshall saw many glinting in the murky water as he made his way deep below the surface. As he reached a depth of 12 metres, he saw the body of a man flat on his back looking up towards the surface. Cast in a macabre posture and trussed up in blue nylon rope, the 13-stone man had been weighed down and gutted. His arms were crossed and his hands had been severed.

PC Marshall later recalled the first chilling hours of what was to be the most brutal and shocking case he had ever seen:

"It started as just another ordinary job," he remembered. "When we got there, there were a few more people on the banks and it seemed something out of the ordinary, a little bit different. We went out on a dinghy and went in over the side. Twelve metres down, there he was, looking up at us. He was flat on his back looking at the sky. His hands and legs were bound and under silt but he had been gutted.

"It became macabre as we realised it was an execution. I will never forget it. But you can't sit and dwell on it or you would not be fit for the job. It is notorious. Lancashire was a sleepy place in those days. You only have to mention the handless corpse and everyone remembers it."

As PC Marshall hauled the victim to the shore, it became clear Eccleston Delph was never supposed to have given up its gruesome secret. But the body of the mystery man, later dubbed Mr Asia because of his eastern connections, had never reached its intended destination at the bottom of the quarry. Thrown from a nearby cliff, the body had been weighed down with coal bags filled with a car jack, weights, bolts and other items. But as it sank through the waters it had become wedged on a shallow ledge below the surface, close to a sunken Mini estate car.

Eccleston Delph.

Detectives were keen to ensure the body was brought up intact, so PC Marshall was tasked to wrap ropes underneath the torso and inch it steadily to the surface. The painstaking operation took two hours before he paddled across to an embankment and placed the body in the shallows.

It was immediately apparent to detectives on the bank that the victim had been subjected to a chilling and cold-blooded execution wildly at odds with the pretty Lancashire visitor attraction where he had been dumped. Investigators quickly assumed it was a gruesome gangland killing and so began the largest and what was to be the most wide-ranging investigation embarked upon by Lancashire Police at the time.

Their first task, to identify who the mysterious dead man was, proved easier said than done. More than 90 officers were put on the case under Detective Superintendent Ray Rimmer, second-in-command of Lancashire CID. But as well as the dismembered hands, the victim's face had been disfigured and he had been shot in the head. He had deep axe wounds to his stomach and his body had been sliced up repeatedly.

> **❝ Around his neck was a distinctive and rare medallion... ❞**

But the 'Handless Corpse', as he was dubbed by the press and public, did divest one secret. Around his neck was a distinctive and rare medallion with a pale blue enamel background inscribed with a gold-coloured Chinese motif. Ironically the message around his neck translated as 'long life'.

The Chinese 'Long Life' blue medallion found on the body of Marty Johnstone.

Armed with this first break in the case, police called a press conference revealing for the first time some of the gruesome details of the find, including the point-blank shooting and the dismembered body. At the centre of their appeal was a plea for information to identify the bronzed, athletically built and once-handsome victim, who they estimated to be aged between 25 and 30. "Anyone who recognises this medallion should contact us immediately," Det Supt Rimmer told the packed media briefing at Chorley police station, announcing a special hotline number.

But a week later, police were still scratching their heads. Police frogmen had made a detailed, but ultimately fruitless, search of the scene to try to find the man's severed hands and a murder weapon. A dental specialist had been called in and Home Office pathologist Dr Geoffrey Garrett carried out a post mortem examination. House-to-house inquiries took place and missing persons' records were scoured but no-one fitted the description.

Officers took the unusual step of issuing a montage picture of the bearded corpse created by police photographers and artists, after deep debate about whether the move could be considered distasteful. They received a barrage of calls from the public who thought they recognised the face of the mystery man. But to no avail. A second photo was issued, this time clean shaven and with a different hairstyle. Then an appeal was put out to the dead man's wife or girlfriend. "Somewhere a girl waits and worries," read the headline in the *Lancashire Evening Post.*

Task Force boss, Superintendent Phil Cafferty, told the newspaper, "He was suntanned and in very good shape. He has got to be some girl's dream man." But in the Chorley CID enquiry room, the handless corpse remained an enigma. On November 29, 1979, the anonymous Mr Asia was buried at Chorley in front of just two mourners while the colossal police murder investigation attracted all the attention.

Then, finally, a breakthrough. It was a phone call from the mother of a young lady called Julie Hue that was to change everything. Phoning from Leyland, she admitted her daughter was Mr Asia's girlfriend, and within hours the scale of the criminal activity became clear.

The dead man was New Zealander Martin 'Marty' Johnstone, a major player in international drugs smuggling and a member of a ruthless drugs syndicate, known as the Kiwi Connection, which operated across Australia, New Zealand, Singapore and Thailand.

The picture of the murder victim circulated by police to identify the corpse.

Julie had been convinced that her boyfriend was in New York at the time of his death, and that she had been taken away to Benidorm by one of the gangster's girlfriends to stop her asking awkward questions. That woman was Barbara Pilkington and she, overcome with guilt, told Julie everything. After flying back to the UK they blew the whistle on the syndicate's entire operation. It emerged than Marty Johnstone had been using illegal passports to travel the world, setting up drug deals while living the high life.

As the investigation unfolded, the constabulary gained a remarkable insight into the world of international drug trafficking. It became apparent that, from the early 1970s, Marty Johnstone had used his menswear business in Auckland as a front to make drug runs back and forth to Thailand. He became friends with Leyland man

Andy Maher who, by 1978, was paying associates to move drugs and money in and out of Britain.

Soon both men became involved with ruthless underworld boss Alexander Sinclair, also known as Terry Clark, who liked to see himself as the 'Al Capone of New Zealand'. But Johnstone enraged Sinclair by short-changing him and diluting supplies of heroin. He was a bungling criminal and was increasingly viewed as a liability to the syndicate. He once made a drugs run to Thailand where he was conned out of £500,000 with bags of sugar – a disaster which saw Maher and Johnstone clash in a Bangkok hotel room. The rest of the gang thought Johnstone smoked too much cannabis and his ineptitude eventually sealed his fate.

By September 1979, Sinclair made it clear to Maher that Johnstone had to be disposed of. Sinclair explained quite calmly to Maher, of Moss Side, Leyland, that if he did not do the deed his girlfriend and child would be 'snuffed out' instead. Maher returned to the north west and called Johnstone in Singapore. He told him that he was needed to complete a syndicate deal in Glasgow. Within two months Johnstone was to be at the bottom of the Delph.

Maher's cousin, James Smith, was telephoned in Scotland and told to come down 'as soon as he could' to Leyland. The killers were planning to murder Johnstone on the way up to Scotland and they wanted Julie Hue out of the way. They also argued over where to dump the corpse afterwards. But when Johnstone announced that he was going to arrive early at Preston train station on October 7, Maher did not have a gun.

Andy Maher's new town home in Robin Hey.

So Terry Sinclair handed 17-year-old babysitter Karen Pidgeon a .38 calibre revolver in a brown paper bag and put her on a train to Preston from London. The daughter of Sylvester Pidgeon, Sinclair's chauffeur, she had taken the £80 first-class trip "for a bit of a lark". She got off the train, handed the parcel to Smith and then caught the next train back to London. Maher's partner, Barbara Pilkington, was told to convince Julie Hue that her boyfriend had been called to New York on business. Meanwhile, Maher set off in his black Jaguar saloon from Leyland to Scotland with Smith in the backseat and Johnstone in the passenger seat. He stopped the car in a lay-by near Carnforth, Lancaster, and, claiming tiredness, leaned over to ask Johnstone if he would drive. Johnstone agreed but as he got out of the car Maher blasted him twice, at point blank range, in the head.

Smith and Maher then drove to a lock-up in Leyland where they cut off Johnstone's hands with an axe and smashed his face with a lump hammer. They also slashed his stomach with the axe in the belief that he would not float when they ditched his body –hacking through his bones so ferociously that it left indentations in the concrete of a vault sunk into the garage floor where the dismembering was carried out.

The lay-by at Skew Bridge north of Carnforth where Johnstone was killed.

Police said they found the walls and floor splattered with blood after they raided the garage. They also discovered Thai sticks – pieces of cannabis from Thailand – and drug-dealing paraphernalia, including scales containing heroin, 2,300 plastic bags, a press for moulding cannabis into bars, a large brown zip-up suitcase with two secret compartments built into its walls, and additional cases of heroin and cannabis ready for transportation. After the killing, the murderers rolled Johnstone's naked body into the flooded Delph Quarry with more than 140lbs of weights strapped to his legs.

By midnight the following day Maher had telephoned Pilkington to tell her "it's done". But the trussed-up body had become wedged on an underwater ledge and was found only five days later by the divers. When Maher saw a newspaper report about the discovery of the body, he calmly reassured Pilkington that no-one could connect it with them. Pilkington then took Julie Hue to Benidorm to get her out of the way of the investigation. However, on their return from Spain they phoned the police, handing detectives the key to an incredible underworld that spanned the globe.

On October 30 at 7.30am, officers burst into Sinclair's luxury flat in London and arrested him and his glamorous lawyer girlfriend at gunpoint. Only later it became clear that the ruthless man at the top of the Kiwi Connection had ordered the killings of at least 10 others during the 1970s. At the time of his arrest, he had accumulated more than £390m from his operation. In all, 12 people faced trial on charges relating to Johnstone's murder and drug trafficking.

Following the completion of a police investigation, an historic 123-day trial was launched at Lancaster Castle starting on January 6, 1981. From the start there was nothing straightforward about the court proceedings as they opened under the spooky shadow of a witch's curse. Superstitious lawyers voiced concerns that the medieval castle courthouse was jinxed, a belief dating back more than 400 years to when the infamous Lancashire witches were tried and hanged in Lancaster Castle. The curse was thought to have reared its head in 1975 when the top security trial of the Birmingham pub bombers was plagued by illness and interruption.

But the court, housed in the hill-top fortress, was considered one of only six court buildings in the country secure enough to house the hearing. A £100,000 security operation was mounted at the castle, including police marksmen with high-powered rifles patrolling the grounds and battlements as well as guarding

Johnstone's business card.

the courtrooms. Other officers with dogs and wearing special thermal suits to keep them warm in sub-zero temperatures, paced the grounds day and night.

The most sophisticated 'magic eye' electronic equipment, similar to that used at airports, was used to scan everyone entering the building – including the country's top barristers, prison officers, reporters and the public. In addition, every individual entering the building was searched six times, including two full body searches, making many of the barristers including six Queen's Counsel, late on the very first day. Bullet-proof windows were specially fitted and binoculars trained on every person entering or leaving the building. Meanwhile, traffic restrictions were put in force on roads leading to the castle.

Only 12 relatives – one for each defendant – were allowed in the court at any one time. A total of 31 desks were built especially for the world's press and in Lancaster itself, hotels and guest houses were booked out, with tradesmen experiencing a mini tourism boom. Trial judge Mrs Justice Heilbron, known as 'Rose of the Bailey', was assigned five policemen to guard her around the clock.

With all these measures in place, 15 months after the New Zealander Johnstone's corpse was found in the Delph, the trial went ahead, with the 12 defendants seated in a specially extended dock in the Castle's semi-circular Gothic Shire Hall. More than 130 witnesses from around the world accounted for almost 2,000 pages of evidence at the trial, running up costs of around £1,000 an hour in legal fees.

Day One: In the courtroom the 'jinx' fears proved to be justified, with the trial lurching from drama to drama, starting just eight minutes in on day one when barristers complained that the rigorous security checks had left them unable to brief their clients. Justice Heilbron called a recess to allow them to do so.

Day Two: Proceedings were halted after just two minutes to discuss technical hitches when the defendants complained they couldn't hear and the lawyers said they didn't have space to take notes. Fresh modifications were ordered to lower the specially-built dock.

Day Three: The trial suffered more problems with defendant Sinclair staging a handcuff protest after complaining about being manacled to a police officer. He wanted to be "treated as a man, not an animal", said Mr Robin Simpson QC at the time, adding, "If this sounds emotive I make no apology because this is what he feels." But Mrs Justice Heilbron refused to change court procedure, also refusing a legal application to split the trial into two parts, one for drugs and one for murder.

Day Four: Finally, on January 13, a jury of seven men and five women was sworn in, as five men, two from Lancashire, pleaded not guilty to murder of international drugs racketeer Marty Johnstone. Those pleading not guilty to murdering Mr Asia included 27-year-old Andrew Mayer, of Leyland; Keith William 'Billy' Kirby, 27, of Clayton Brook near Preston; Alexander Sinclair, 36, of Kensington, London; James Smith, of Livingstone; and Frederick Russell, of Kentish Town, London.

Day Five: The jinx struck again when the 12 members of the jury, only elected the day before, were dramatically ordered to stand down. Another jury was sworn in, with Mrs Justice Heilbron explaining the move was for 'technical reasons' that she could not explain at the time. It later emerged that one male juror had 'tenuous' connections to a clerk at a law firm in the case and another had been seen speaking to a policeman on duty outside the castle. So 60 new potential jurors were brought to the castle and seven men and five women – the same make-up as the original jury – were selected.

Day Six: The delays, and the cost of those delays, were making headlines of their own. The then MP for Ormskirk, and later to be television presenter, Robert Kilroy-Silk, asked the Attorney General Sir Michael Havers to make public the cost of the Mr Asia trial, which had so far passed without a single piece of evidence being heard. He added, "I would have thought there were more effective ways of dealing with the preliminaries without this enormous disruption."

Finally, case evidence began to be heard at the court. Prosecuting Counsel Michael Maguire QC told the trial that the house garage in Leyland "looked like a slaughterhouse" after Marty Johnstone was brutally killed. He described horrifying mutilations to the body in an attempt to avoid

The axe used by Andrew Maher to cut off Johnstone's hands.

identification and how the murdered man was a "senior member of an international drugs syndicate, peddling misery and slow death across Australia, New Zealand, the United States and Britain." But he urged the jury that this was no justification for murder, "We are not here to make moral judgements."

Marty Johnstone, who had pioneered the UK end of the syndicate, was in the way. He had to be removed. "There was nothing personal about it. It was simply a matter of business. They all loved him, he stood high, wide and handsome throughout the world, spending his money."

He said Sinclair had told Maher, Johnstone had to go. "It may well be that it was put in such a way that if Johnstone did not go, Maher would go," added Mr Maguire. So Maher phoned Johnstone in Singapore and told him he was needed in Scotland for a deal. "But it was a lie and a charade," said Mr Maguire. Maher booked Johnstone and his girlfriend one-way tickets from Singapore. "Emphasis on the one way – they didn't want to waste money," said Mr Maguire. As their prey set off on his final journey, Maher's old school friend, defendant Kirby, was out shopping for the axe, the weights and the hammer.

Day Seven: By this point the details of the elaborate plot were becoming clear to the court. It emerged drugs syndicate bosses were considering cleaning up all the loose ends and that included murdering Johnstone's girlfriend Julie Hue. They feared the Leyland girl would start asking questions – so to get her out the way she was taken to Spain by the common-law wife of Andrew Maher, the man who shot 'Mr Asia'.

With Julie out the way Maher and Smith drove to Scotland "their hands bloodied from their task" in a car "soiled with the blood of their victim". In a parcel they carried their victim's amputated hands and the revolver used to 'snuff out' his life. When they arrived in Scotland they met syndicate member Kingsley Fagan who helped them to clear the car of blood. "It was an impossible task because there was so much blood, but they worked hard at it," said Mr Maguire.

Documents belonging to Johnstone were burned, and the hands wrapped in a brown paper envelope before being thrown into the River Almond. The revolver was smashed with a hammer and thrown into a nearby quarry. The seat covers of the Jaguar car, badly bloodstained, were left on a rubbish tip. Later Maher phoned his partner Barbara Pilkington in Leyland and told her to clean up any blood visible on the door of their garage.

After his return from Scotland, Maher, with the help of Kirby, attempted to clean the garage further and cover the floor with cement. Kirby later delivered a parcel, including bloodstained clothing, the axe and the hammer to his father's home in Ingol, Preston. But he made a crucial mistake, failing to remove the Chinese medallion from the dead man's body, despite the specific instructions of Maher.

It was at this point of the trial, on January 17, that it became apparent just how much power was held by the members of the drugs syndicate. Its members 'bought' Customs Officers and had lawyers in their pockets, with one man, known as 'Mr Big' or 'The Ace', having the power to say who lived – and who died. That man was Terry Clarke, aka Alexander James Sinclair.

Prosecutor Mr Maguire told the Lancaster Castle trial that syndicate members used false passports like 'confetti'. Normally bought in Thailand, drugs were initially shipped to Australia and New Zealand and later carried by girl couriers on flights to Singapore. The girl couriers at first carried the drugs strapped to their bodies. Later they used false-bottomed suitcases with the powdered drugs in glass-fibre blocks to avoid sniffer dogs.

They also organised runs to Fiji and the USA. Couriers usually carried the drugs in two big tartan-patterned suitcases at a time, with an average street value of £1.5m. Mr Maguire said, "This syndicate had lawyers in their pockets in Australia and New Zealand. They bought, here and there, the odd Customs Officer."

But the house of cards fell apart when, back home in England, Barbara Pilkington showed remorse for the first time. In Benidorm she had confessed to Julie, who was fretting after not hearing from Marty on her birthday, that her man had, in fact, been murdered. On their return to the UK they told Julie's mother what they knew and she contacted police. Mr Maguire told the court that one of those arrested was Sinclair, who used several aliases and was immensely wealthy. He would provide finance to buy off officials – he was undoubtedly Mr Asia's boss.

Day Eight: Even more gruesome details were emerging from the trial. The court heard that a hidden safe filled with drugs marked the bloody spot where Johnstone was hacked to pieces by his friends in the Leyland lock-up. Maher himself was on the run in Singapore when the raid took place, flying out of the country when Johnstone's body was pulled out of the Delph. Meanwhile, other important syndicate members headed to a crisis meeting at a hotel in Hastings, to ensure supplies of heroin from Singapore should not be interrupted after their link – Mr Asia – was 'taken out'.

> **"** ...Johnstone was hacked to pieces by his friends... **"**

But one syndicate member who could not make the meeting was Errol Hincksman. He had been arrested in Bexhill the previous day and breathalysed. Police found traces of cannabis on him and the passport of a Chinaman. One officer had even joked unwittingly with him: "For all we know you may be an international drugs smuggler!" He was released and picked up two days later at the home of 'Mr Big' Sinclair and his lawyer girlfriend in Kensington, who were in bed together in the luxurious apartment when police swooped.

Days later and homes, houses and premises used by the syndicate were being raided. In one house in Finchley, the home of 'banker' Leila Barclay, police found a large amount of property belonging to Sinclair, drugs and forged passports. The house was described by Mr Maguire as an 'Aladdin's Cave'.

Meanwhile, the murderers' cover-up efforts had been scuppered again, after massacred Johnstone's hand was found 'almost by a miracle' by a diver in the fast-flowing River Almond in Scotland. It still bore the victim's fingerprints. The frogman had made the macabre find after he "trod on something soft" trapped between stones on the riverbed. Later, the gun used to kill Johnstone was found in a quarry in Scotland after 11 million gallons of water were pumped out.

Day Nine: Revelations that the teenager carried the murder weapon from London to Preston were told to the court. Karen Pidgeon said she completed the sinister delivery at Preston Railway Station, "No-one told me what was in the parcel I was carrying. I was there for about six minutes. Dad asked me if I would mind carrying a parcel for Terry to Preston." She told the jury she was driven to Euston station by her father – chauffeur to Sinclair – who was also in the car. But traffic was heavy and she missed the train she was supposed to catch, eventually boarding an hour later.

Sinclair, who had been paying Karen £40 a week to look after his 11-year-old daughter Angie in London, gave her £80. She carried the long, narrow, parcel in her shoulder bag before arriving in Preston, explaining why she was a late to a man who was "a bit chubby" before accompanying him to his car, then catching the next train back to London. She told the jury this man was Maher.

As Maher languished in his cell during the trial, it seems his conscience started to kick in. Desperate to justify himself, he told his father, former Preston pub landlord Martin Maher, "I don't want you to think I'm some sort of monster. My life and the lives of Barbara and the baby were in danger." His dad told the court they were his son's exact words. And the next day – a breakthrough. In a sensational move, Maher dramatically admitted murdering Marty Johnstone. Despite his previous denials, he stood in the dock and said firmly, "Guilty".

The world's press reeled with the news, which quickly reverberated around the globe.

It was January 22, and as Maher contemplated a certain future behind bars, the trial continued. Next up in the witness box was his girlfriend Barbara Pilkington, 24, who told the court of tensions within the drugs ring. Given immunity from prosecution after turning Queen's Evidence, Barbara said Maher had been called a 'fool' on more than one occasion for sticking with Johnstone. Others in the syndicate were dissatisfied with the way he was doing business and that he smoked too much cannabis. But Maher believed in Johnstone, despite his continuing bungles.

Speaking slowly and deliberately, the pretty and petite brunette told how she had lived with Maher since 1978. They had first met in the Windsor Castle pub in Preston, then run by Maher's father. It had been some time before she had realised his real business was drugs. "As far as I was aware it was an import and export business of furniture and tropical fish."

Later she admitted helping to lure Johnstone to his death in Lancashire. She booked the dead man's one-way ticket from Singapore, knowing he was going to be murdered. But, when her lover Maher asked her on the eve of the killing, "Am I doing the right thing?" she had replied, "Do you have to be the one to kill him?"

At midnight the next day Maher had phoned her at home and said "It's done." She said that Johnstone had once tried to use her and her baby Martia as couriers, but Maher had refused to allow it.

Day 12: Next up in the box was the beautiful blonde girlfriend of the murdered man. Dubbed the 'bathing beauty' by the press, who repeatedly ran pictures of her posing by a pool, Julie Hue – a former Leyland beauty queen – was brought to court under a heavy police escort after 15 months in protective police custody. She, like Barbara Pilkington, had been granted immunity from prosecution and would live her life under a new identity after the case.

She told how she met the handsome New Zealander Marty Johnstone in April 1979, six months before his butchered body was found. They later became lovers. Earlier the court heard of a death threat against Julie from a senior member of the drugs syndicate. She described how she invented a sick relative to get a passport quickly before travelling to Singapore after visits to see some of the syndicate members. "At that time I had no idea that Martin was dealing in drugs," she claimed.

But later, at a beach chalet in Thailand, she told how she was asked to stand guard while syndicate members 'messed' about with weights in suitcases and how, at the London flat of Sinclair, she heard a conversation about a parcel to be delivered to Singapore. She had seen Johnstone unload canvas money bags with cash into a suitcase and once saw Sinclair borrow glasses from his chauffeur to have his passport photo taken. She admitted passing on messages and parcels of money and spoke of how members of the syndicate had taken cocaine in London. She also described 'Mr Big' Sinclair travelling in disguise on a plane, dying his hair, moustache and eyebrows but absentmindedly wiping his face and smudging the make-up. But the memories proved too painful for Julie, who broke down in the witness box as she remembered her former lover. The 23-year-old had to be helped from the courtroom in tears and when the judge heard she was 'too distressed' to continue, the courtroom was temporarily adjourned.

The tearful woman was asked to relive the night in Leyland she waved goodbye to her lover, thinking he was en route to a drugs meeting in Scotland. Instead he was driven off to meet his grisly death. She was shown Maher's gold watch and his monogrammed briefcase. Then she was handed the Chinese medallion found round his neck when police hauled his butchered body from the water.

Her last memory – she told the court – was of him sitting in the front passenger seat of Maher's Jaguar being driven off into the night. It was the car in which he would later die. Asked by Mr Charles Mantell QC, for the prosecution, "Did you ever see him alive again?" she sobbed, "No." Moments later she slumped on the side of the witness box, weeping.

Terry Sinclair, the drugs mastermind.

Next in the dock was Scotsman James Smith who witnessed the brutal killing of Johnstone. "I nearly died of shock myself," he told police after they arrived at his home. "It was like a nightmare. I wish I had never seen Leyland."

He described the car trip to Scotland with his cousin, ex-marine Maher, that was to be Johnstone's last. He said they got lost in Lancaster city centre and stopped near the bus station for directions. Then, about 20 minutes north on the A6 out of the city, Maher had pulled out the revolver and shot Johnstone at close range in the head. "The noise was deafening. I felt stunned. I hadn't expected Andy to do it so quickly."

He said Maher had asked him to carry out the killing but he refused. "It's no good saying aye and then when the time comes, not being able to do."

He told how the body was put in the passenger seat of the car where Maher stabbed him in the stomach, adding, "By this time our bottles had gone."

Later they changed into overalls for the gruesome task of chopping up the body in the Leyland garage, stripping the corpse, smashing the face and tying on weights. He said that when asked by Maher to smash the face with a hammer, he said, "I couldn't go through with it. I felt sick."

So Maher took over and pulverised Johnstone's features. Smith said, "I think he was just about cracking up. Just then a car pulled up outside the garage. It just about destroyed us. That was me finished. To this day I don't know how we managed to get the body in the car boot or how we didn't wake anybody up with the noise we were making."

Some days later in Leyland, Maher had shown him cuttings from the *Lancashire Evening Post*. They went for a drink and spent time "just kidding each other how we would get away with it". He added, "When it comes to it we can't justify what we did. I got involved because I kept thinking of Barbara and the child and Andy led me to believe Martin had authorised killings in the past."

Andrew Maher, hitman in the Mr Asia case.

Next evidence to be heard was that of barmaid Maureen McKeown, from Ormskirk, who told how a joke and a glass of champagne nearly turned very sour for her and the accused. She was working at the Piper nightclub when Maher and Smith rolled up, after drinking at the nearby Jolly Farmer and Boars Head pubs. Also out that night was another defendant, Kingsley Fagan, accused of drugs offences. What happened put the three men in a panic. The waitress, after watching them flash their cash and ask for a bottle of champagne, jokingly asked them if they were spending the 'pay-off' money for the murder. "I nearly fainted," said Smith. Mrs McKeown asked them what they were celebrating and was told, "Nothing." She said, "It was at that point I made a rather dreadful remark to him.I told them, 'I wish I could celebrate nothing. You haven't done that murder in Chorley have you?'"

One of the men had asked, "What murder is that?" and after being told, said, "We don't know about that."

"I said, 'you must do, it's in all the papers.'" Later, the men had asked another member of staff if she was a policewoman and then invited Mrs McKeown to a party. Luckily, she refused the invitation.

Into February, and the trial saw the prosecution outline their case against joiner Billy Kirby, of Daisy Meadow, Clayton Brook. The court heard that, in statements, he said he lied to police about his involvement with the drugs syndicate because he was "frightened to death". When he eventually admitted buying weights and a rope to conceal Mr Asia's body, the 27-year-old told police, "He ended up with a bullet in the head and it could be me and the wife next. If I tell you anything, I could end up dead."

> **"** If I tell you anything, I could end up dead. **"**

He said he had been recruited by old school pal Maher and employed for up to £1,000 a month to make false compartments in suitcases used for drug smuggling, describing himself as a 'small cog' in the organisation. Later he admitted going on a £40 shopping spree in Preston, at the request of Maher, buying weights, nylon, a hand axe, a hammer and a rope before the killing, and helping dispose of bloodstained objects afterwards.

He claimed his old school friend told him, "If it ever got to court the witnesses would never see the light of day to give evidence." As the murder took place, Kirby fled to Cumbria, later being called back to help Maher clean up the garage where the butchering had taken place. "Andy couldn't do it and it nearly made me sick," he told police. "The blood was all thick and clotted. I made a concrete mix with it and shovelled it into a bag. I swilled the rest out with water the best I could."

He then took a trunk filled with bloodstained articles to his father's house in Ingol, Preston. His father had burned them and some of ashes had been thrown into a brook at the bottom of the garden. After his arrest he tried to justify his actions, saying, "What could I do? If I hadn't done that it could have been me that got shot."

But he admitted Andy had told him to get rid of the Chinese medallion from the body – which he failed to do. "He told me to make sure of destroying the chain. He said it was important but I never saw a chain. To be honest I didn't look for it. I just burned the lot." Finally, 24 days into the trial, the infamous 'Mr Big' found himself under scrutiny, as the prosecution evidence was outlined. Having told police he was worth a staggering 50 million New Zealand dollars, he was asked how he made his money. "I don't know," he had replied, "I have people advising me how to invest. Money makes money all the time." He later claimed to have won vast sums at roulette and at the stock market to explain large sums of cash at his flat.

He finally admitted to paying off officials across the world, including narcotics squad officers in Australia and New Zealand, having telephones bugged and computers and telex machines tapped. Asked why Mr Asia had been murdered, he told officers at Chorley police station, "I can guess. Look, you live on the knife edge in this game. There is always someone ready to take over. If you die, you die. In this game you can go at any time. I wake up each morning and say good morning day, and if I wake up the next day and say 'good morning' again, I think I'm lucky."

During interrogation by police, he had commented, "You guys could write a book on me. If you do though I want a cut of the royalties." He said that even when he had been under arrest previously on what he claimed was a "trumped up charge," his business kept ticking over nicely. "I have plenty of money to buy a blind eye or two." He refused to take the blame for Maher killing Johnstone, saying, "That's down to Andy. He killed him. I couldn't force him, could I?" He claimed he talked Maher out of killing Julie Hue, "I knew Andy was going to shoot Martin, but Christ, I talked him out of killing Julie."

Next under the microscope was Mr Big's beautiful lawyer girlfriend, Karen Soich, 24. In statements to police she described her day-to-day life in Britain as the lover of the drugs syndicate king as "disco dancing, gambling, cooking and stocking up provisions for the

Karen Soich.

house, making love and sleeping." She told how she once flew to Los Angeles to join Sinclair at a hotel where there were "lots and lots" of Cadillacs, how he put 10,000 Australian dollars in a bank account for her to cover travelling costs if he ever asked her to join him, and how he would give her £100 stake money every time they went gambling in Ladbrokes in London. "If I won I had to give back the £100 and keep the winnings. I won something like £2,300."

But the dark haired barrister from New Zealand denied knowing Sinclair was a drug dealer, although she admitted she suspected his dealings were not 'whiter than white'. She said that although she had known him 18 months, they had only actually spent 11 weeks together. Then Soich – who denied two drug conspiracy charges – said she met Sinclair when she represented him in a case in which he was acquitted. While being questioned by police she refused to divulge details of that case, saying it was "privileged information between lawyer and client", to which Det Sgt Halsall had replied "Rubbish! We're talking about murder, not a traffic offence."

Later, the court heard, she shouted out to her lover – who was also in the police station – in a loud voice, "I love you Terry, I am still with you." Next witness for the prosecution was American 'pimp and pusher' Benjie Bennett who drove to the Beverley Hilton Hotel in LA with cocaine stashed in his socks. The court was told how he feared he was being set up by undercover police but when his contact – a New Zealander called Terry – seemed insulted and started pulling out bank statements totalling 'multiples of millions', he was convinced he was genuine.

'Terry' was in fact Sinclair and he met Mr Bennett, who drove a white Rolls Royce, in the cocktail bar of the plush hotel, before the pair sat down for drinks at a table of four or five men and a woman. Bennett said he accompanied 'Terry' to his suite of rooms upstairs where he was introduced to a dark-haired woman called Karen, who also spoke with a New Zealand accent. Here, Mr Bennett agreed to snort 'a little' cocaine and drank vodka, after overcoming initial worries that Karen was a cop.

The court heard how the pimp's sordid life had undergone a remarkable transformation in the wake of the Mr Asia arrests. After peddling slow death on the streets of LA, the 30-year-old sometime drug addict became a drug abuse counsellor, giving up his stable of call girls and turning his back on crime altogether. Asked why he had joined the fight against drugs, he said, "It's crucial in the States that the drug flow be cut down to a minimal amount. It's killing too many people."

Despite his fervour, he was accused of "lying his head off" by Mr Simpson QC, to which he replied, "Well, that's for you to suggest."

The trial was now 30 days in and it was time for another dramatic confession. Twenty days after Maher's admission, Londoner Freddie Russell, who had already pleaded guilty to two charges of conspiracy to supply and import stolen drugs, pleaded guilty when the murder indictment was put in front of him again. He had acquired the gun and ammunition used for the execution and it was claimed had 'little love' for Marty Johnstone, who had double crossed him and caused his 'street name' to be tarnished. Prosecution QC Mr Maguire had earlier said Russell was under the influence of syndicate banker Leila Barclay, his girlfriend of 20 years.

Next the court heard the story of high-flying courier Kay Reynolds, who risked her life to help move drugs around the world, one of a bevy of beautiful girls used by the syndicate. The red-headed Australian was recruited in Sydney, where she worked in a massage , to fly to Singapore and return with a consignment of heroin. But when she arrived she was met in Singapore by Maher, who told her the plan had changed and she had to fly to England.

Riches and risk went hand in hand for Reynolds, who was paid about £1,000 for two hours' work, but knew she faced the death penalty if caught smuggling drugs out of Bangkok. "I was very scared," she admitted, but said she did it anyway, stuffing drugs into false-bottomed suitcases. She explained that couriers always flew economy class but were shadowed by escorts, who always flew in first class.

Day 56: Reynolds named two lawyers as the men the syndicate turned to in times of trouble. She had been given the names – Ian Strathdee and Mr P.C. Williams - in case a smuggling operation went

Marty Johnstone, aka Mr Asia.

wrong. The courier also said the syndicate had a series of airport signals to avoid direct contact between escort and courier: "If a shoulder bag was carried on the right arm, everything was OK. If it was on the left arm there was trouble. If there was trouble, the person waiting outside the customs gate had to ring the lawyers."

"Killer, help me or I'll blame you," said the headline on day 70 of the Handless Corpse trial. The court heard that 15 years of friendship meant nothing in the desperate days that followed the murder of Mr Asia. Killer Andrew Maher threatened his boyhood pal Billy Kirby, "Help me clean up or I'll tell the police on you."

In the witness box Kirby said he was given the ultimatum near the bloodstained garage at Leyland, where the corpse was butchered. He admitted previously buying weights, rope and an axe for Maher, claiming he was unaware of their purpose, thinking they were for use of 'disposing of a batch of bad cannabis'. He took Maher and Smith to the edge of the Eccleston Delph, where the handless corpse was later dumped.

He said it was only in an argument with Maher at his Leyland home that he found out the truth: "At first I thought it was April Fool's Day. I thought it was a bit of a sick joke. But he convinced me it was serious. He was really frightened."

After escaping to Cumbria he returned to help clean up the bloody garage, saying, "Andy told me I was involved. He told me Martin was at the bottom of the Delph wearing things that I had bought."

On Kirby's behalf, Mr John Hugill QC argued the 28-year-old was an accessory after the fact, saying, "He is not guilty of the actual crime of murder."

Day 69: Once again the police were in the firing line, with detectives being called 'bloody liars'. Sinclair told the court that interviews had been 'twisted' and that his interrogators drew up inaccurate statements without a single note being taken. The outburst came on the second day of Sinclair's statement from the dock. He elected not to testify under oath for fear of being 'busted' in New Zealand for any sworn evidence.

He denied Johnstone had been killed for double-crossing him, claiming, "Nothing can be further from the truth. Marty was my friend. He was not ripping me off." He denied telling police he was worth 50 million dollars, and that he had corrupt officials in his pocket. But he did admit lying under interrogation about knowing Errol Hincksman, saying, "I wasn't going to turn into Bertie Small and grass on everyone I knew."

Finally, 150 witnesses later, the trial had reached day 65 and the Crown had completed its case in the Mr Asia trial. The end appeared to be in sight. But there was more to come. On May 2, Hincksman, facing charges of conspiring to supply and import drugs, spoke out in his own defence, completing an unsworn statement. He said his 'wrongful arrest' for murder was the most frightening experience of his life: "I was lost, lonely and bloody frightened." The Crown had described him as the 'right hand and trusted aide' of Sinclair, but he had denied having any involvement in murder.

Karen Soichs also disputed the prosecution evidence. She told the court, "I guess what it boils down to is I am facing charges of smuggling drugs into this country and supplying drugs in this country and there is no way I am guilty of either of these charges."

June 16, day 100, and finally Mrs Justice Heilbron was due to start summing up. Fourteen days later – on day 115, July 7 – she finally completed. On day 123, after 140 hours of deliberation, the jury returned with a unanimous verdict. And so, the end of a trial dogged with controversy and incident. But finally, justice was done.

" The jury returned with a unanimous verdict. "

Three men were found guilty of murdering Marty Johnstone: Preston joiner Billy Kirby, Scotsman James Smith and multi-millionaire syndicate owner, Terry Sinclair. They awaited their sentence alongside Andrew Maher of Leyland and Freddie Russell from London, who had admitted their guilt earlier. Three more syndicate members, Errol Hincksman of New Zealand, chauffeur Sylvestor Pidgeon and Christopher Blackman were all found guilty of drug offences. But three defendants were acquitted, including former Scots guard Kingsley Fagan, who had spent more than 20 months in custody only to be declared innocent. The others, accountant Jack Barclay and Karen Soich, had been on bail virtually throughout.

Miss Soich and Mr Barclay were the only defendants to show emotion at their acquittal. Sinclair, despite being convicted and facing an inevitable life sentence, was still able to smile smugly at the jury's damning decision. A 12th defendant, Jack's mother Leila Barclay, also awaited a sentence for two counts of drugs conspiracy after pleading guilty before the trial.

Following the decision, Mrs Justice Heilbron said the constabulary's Det Supt Rimmer and his team deserved praise for their "brilliant, painstaking and successful investigation" which saw police sergeants jetting across the globe to unpick the various chains in the deadly heroin smuggling ring operation.

Julie Hue and Barbara Pilkington revealed details of the syndicate's whole operation to the court as witnesses for the prosecution. In return Pilkington, then 24, and Hue were both granted immunity from prosecution. Since the trial, the pair have been living new lives with new identities.

In total, nine people were jailed for their involvement in the killing of Marty Johnstone and a variety of drug offences. Maher was caged for life with a recommendation he serve at least 20 years. He was later taken out of the prison system under the Mental Health Act of 1983 and eventually sectioned in Merseyside's Ashworth secure hospital with severe depression. He is now out of custody and thought to live in Lancashire.

His boss, drug baron Sinclair, read books while he sat in the dock in Lancaster Castle. Complacent to the last, he had thought his power would allow him to buy freedom. But he was sentenced to life at top security Parkhurst Prison on the Isle of Wight and ordered to pay £1 million toward prosecution costs. Mrs Justice Heilbron told him, "You pursued an evil trade. There is overwhelming evidence of you being the mastermind behind this most terrible drugs syndicate. You were peddling misery and death."

His attempt to overturn the conviction was dismissed by appeal judges. He died two years later from a heart attack, aged just 39. A fake death theory immediately did the rounds among Lancashire police officers who thought he may have bought his way out of prison. But his body was positively identified.

> **" His attempt to overturn the conviction was dismissed by appeal judges. "**

A fellow inmate in Parkhurst claimed he died during an elaborate bid for freedom, taking an untraceable drug called phytomenadione, smuggled in by a visitor in a glass phial, which induces a fake heart attack. The plan was to then 'spring him' as he arrived for emergency treatment in hospital, it was claimed. But one of the policemen who helped put him behind bars rejected the claims as 'unlikely'. Billy Kirby was imprisoned for life, as were James Smith and Freddie Russell. Four other syndicate members were jailed for a total of 33 years. Leila Barclay was to serve 13 years; Hincksman 10 years; and Blackman and Pidgeon, five years each.

Maher was also ordered to pay £10,000, although the judge said, "Most of your money will never be discovered."

Today, Lancashire police look back on the downfall of one of the world's biggest drug syndicates as 'the most far-reaching criminal case the constabulary has ever dealt with'.

It was only as the court case played out that the true extent of the drug syndicate was made clear. Mind-boggling money behind dealers in dope and death kept the Kiwi Connection in business for more than four years. And what a business it was.

Millions made in a matter of days. A gang of addicts and one-time petty crooks living a life of fabulous luxury. The rewards for loyalty were immense; the price paid for treason even higher. The syndicate silenced squealers with ruthless efficiency. At least a dozen couriers died as triggermen purged the flourishing organisation of security risks. The last to be killed was Marty Johnstone, a victim of the cancerous greed he started spreading five years before.

> **" The syndicate silenced squealers with ruthless efficiency. "**

In 1974 Johnstone had been a hard-up salesman, but by the time he died in 1979 he was worth millions. So too were others who controlled the biggest dope ring Australia has ever known. Conservative estimates put the earnings of the Kiwi Connection in five years at 250 million New Zealand Dollars. Sinclair once bragged he was worth 50 million dollars, give or take a million or two. And police in five countries are still looking for Johnstone's nest egg, hidden away in property, safety deposit boxes and bank accounts under a host of fictitious names around the globe.

One Australian detective with years of big-time crime fighting under his belt could find only these words to describe the size of the operation: "Bloody mind-boggling." A senior officer in England put it another way: "They were spending more on phone calls in a night than we were getting in a month's salary." Mr Asia's millions are still sought by police in five countries who believe his earnings are stashed away in safety deposit boxes, bank accounts and property under false names. But it was Terence Alexander Sinclair who was the biggest fish caught after the macabre discovery in the Eccleston Delph quarry. He was the so-called Angel of Death who offered cunning and corruption as the twin weapons with which to fight the combined police forces of Australasia. But the Angel crashed to earth when police swooped at the posh flat in London that was his 'English connection'.

When Lancashire Police finally broke the operation wide open in 1979 they found it was made up of more than 90 people around the world. Sinclair and a handful of assorted ranks were under lock and key. But the vast majority were free and

rapidly went toground. For a time they left an empire in ruins, addicts without supplies. In New Zealand heroin all but vanished from the streets.

But soon the inevitable battle began for control of what was left. New distributors moved in to push supplies around Australasia. Police in Britain, New Zealand and Australia were justifiably proud to have destroyed one evil supply line. But they know only too well others quickly took its place. For a while, the incredible investigation disrupted supplies of drugs across the world and left a huge drug conglomerate in tatters. And when, several years ago, Eccleston Delph was drained and 250 rusty cars were recovered, it became clear that Mr Asia's handless corpse could easily have been lying among them, had it not been for a bungled cover-up.

The chilling brutality of one of the world's most bloodthirsty drug empires could have remained hidden forever if the freezing black waters of Eccleston Delph had not chosen to divulge their terrible secrets to two divers on that cold autumn day.

CHAPTER FOUR

Twisted justice

William Openshaw, Broughton, May 11, 1981

The crowd of holidaymakers peered anxiously up into the gloom as the slanting rain lashed down on Blackpool's famous Golden Mile. In the distance the sea was grey and choppy, the wind-swept sands deserted in the murk of the early August evening. But it was the height of the 1980 summer season in the popular Lancashire resort and thousands of tourists were making the dash through the showers to the bright lights and curiosities of the promenade. And there was only one attraction on their agenda – the famous Blackpool Tower.

He was first spotted at around 7.30pm. A lone figure, perched perilously at the top of the tower, seemingly oblivious to the spectacle he was creating. Aged around 30 and wearing a one-piece blue flying suit, he had evaded staff by taking the lift with other tourists, before vaulting a locked security gate to the crow's nest. The man, with a scarf wrapped round his face, then climbed to the flagpole close to the pinnacle of the 518ft tower before returning to his perch.

As the crowds of rubberneckers grew on the ground and with the light failing, police beamed powerful floodlights up to the man, who appeared to be making a protest of some kind. It was to be an anxious waiting game.

There the man remained all night, talking to officers positioned on a platform 20ft below him, refusing offers of food or clothing. The next morning a baffled police spokesman told the *Lancashire Evening Post*, "He says he will come down today having made his protest about something which he has done. But we don't know what it is."

He said the man had sent two letters to civil liberties and prisoners' rights organisations before his climb, but his cause was unknown. As the day wore on, the expanding crowd below became impatient, some even drawing messages in the sand urging him to jump. One local man, DJ Gary Wild, even cashed in on the spectacle, charging 10p for three minutes use of his antique telescope. Police looked into summoning the man's sister from her Lancashire home to talk him down. But 41 hours into the protest, after surviving on just two Mars Bars and a bottle of water, the man climbed down from the tower, drawn by a cup of tea and a cigarette. He claimed to have made his point over perceived police brutality and prison conditions.

After being taken to court and bound over to keep the peace, he later admitted the stunt was 'stupid'. His solicitor at the time told the court, "It was the only way he felt he could get himself any degree of notoriety." In fact, the stunt was not a cry for help, it was a statement of intent.

For that man, who had climbed the tower and waved at tourists, was – in just a year's time – to become one of Lancashire's most infamous murderers. The man dubbed the 'Birdman of Blackpool' by the press was in fact 30-year-old John Smith. He was on a mission to serve up his own twisted justice.

But nobody had seen the signs of a maniac 12 years earlier. The scene was Preston Crown Court, 1968, where a petulant, hate-filled teenager glared across the court at the man who had just sent him to Borstal. Then aged just 18, John Smith – a tearaway from Burnley with a violent streak – was in the dock for stealing scrap metal, the latest in a series of petty crimes.

The case was over in an hour. The decision was final. It was an unremarkable case, just one of many in a normal day in a busy court and was to warrant just a small mention in the press. But it was the day that lit the slow-burning touch paper and started

John Smith protesting on Blackpool Tower.

Smith on the road to murder. The grudge was to fester in Smith's troubled mind for 13 years, leaving mental scars that just would not heal.

Filled with anger that day, he memorised the serious but kindly face of the tall be-wigged figure who spoke sternly to him as he ordered the guards to take him below. It was a face he would never forget and a grudge that would rumble on and finally explode in a bloodthirsty frenzy more than a decade later.

The judge was William Openshaw. Father-of-three and a grandfather, Judge William Harrison Openshaw was a rarity – a senior circuit judge who never lost the common touch and earned the love and respect of those who grew close to him. Born in Southport, he was a major in the King's Own Border Regiment during the Second World War, seeing action in North Africa and with the famous Chindits in Burma. He returned to the northern courts circuit as a forthright barrister, becoming chairman of the county's Quarter Sessions in 1958.

Reluctant to appear standoffish or superior, the 6ft 6ins tall 'gentle giant', known to his friends as 'Bill', refused to listen to those who thought it wrong for a judge well-known to the criminal classes to have a home telephone that was not ex-directory. He chose no hiding place – he had nothing to hide – but elected to have his name and address in the telephone book for all to see. He once admitted getting annoying phone calls, saying, "one gets used to it". He told *Lancashire Evening Post* crime reporter Jim Potts in 1979, "My wife is even more used to them than I. The other day a man rang and asked, 'Where's the old so and so now?' My wife, almost without thinking said, 'Oh, he's popping around in the garden.'"

A man of the people and lover of the great outdoors, he would stop in the street to chat about the fortunes of his beloved Preston North End football club, where he was a member of Deepdale's Guild Club. And he played a full role in the civic life of the area as Preston's honorary recorder and a Deputy Lieutenant of Lancashire from 1968. He was also a JP and president of the Preston Marriage Guidance Council. On March 23, 1972, he officially opened the town's new magistrates courts. He became a father figure as well as a senior judge, so much so that in court circles he was nicknamed 'Father'.

Retired court-keeper Beatrice Williams later told the *Evening Post*, "He loved his nickname. After I retired I would see him shopping in Preston Market and would always stop and chat about Preston North End. And he loved his fishing. When we were at the court he would bring the fish he had caught to show my husband."

She recalled his friendly chat and jokes with court staff behind the scenes, "He bought all the ladies a box of chocolates at Christmas. I would go in and chat with him every morning. He was a smashing boss."

The great and good of Lancashire society paid tribute at Judge Openshaw's funeral.

She recalled the day he could not stop laughing after a joke the staff played. When the judge had complained he had no pencil sharpener, unlike a fellow judge, the court staff bought him one and held an unveiling ceremony. "He thought that was hilarious." He was liked and respected for his humorous, understanding nature, coupled with a sense of justice and fair play.

But in court, Judge Openshaw, educated at Harrow and Cambridge and called to the bar in 1936, was not a man to cross. His brand of justice was considered fair and dignified to those on the wrong side of the law. The son of former senior Preston judge Sir James Openshaw, he took a stance against violence, particularly muggings, assaults on police and any attacks where weapons were used. He would say that muggers should be called 'highway robbers' like they were in the old days. It was typical of his personal courage that after falling in the snow and injuring his knee during bad weather, he still carried on with his judicial duties regardless. But as Judge Openshaw continued with his high-flying career, another man was plotting his downfall.

From the moment he was sent to Borstal that day in 1968, John Smith began developing a warped obsession that he was being persecuted by police and the courts. He regularly complained about being beaten in cells and was angered by what he saw as injustice to others. And he saw Judge Openshaw as the man who –

so many years before – had sowed the seeds of his hatred of the law.

Mrs Linda Hargreaves lived next door to Smith for 12 years in Burnley and said he had "lost the plot" after his mother died. Within days of her death he had stolen his first car. She said, "He read over and over books on people like Timothy Evans and James Hanratty. He thought they never

Brownside Road, Worsthorne, near Burnley. John Smith's home for twenty years.

should have been hanged and could get quite angry about it."

Smith's father, Fred, told friends he was worried about his son's "unhealthy obsession". But the old man died of a heart attack, just days after being beaten by Smith during a domestic row. Smith's sister, Brenda Morrison, said, "John developed a pathological hatred of the police. He called them the 'filth' and was always complaining they were getting away with treating people like animals."

It was this obsession that motivated Smith to scale up Blackpool Tower.

But it was not the first time Smith had gone to the top in search of what he believed was justice. His taste for publicity had started far earlier. In 1973 he had to be talked down from a 140ft chimney in Burnley – again in protest over police brutality. A week later he was in court for attacking a stranger in the street. At the time he boasted about breaking into the chambers of a judge and stealing property.

To those who knew him, Smith was a loner. He could not mix easily without drink and had no real friends outside his sister's family. He would spend hours walking alone across the fields around his home village, obsessing and plotting. When the family home was sold after his father's death, Smith began living as a tramp, sleeping rough in an old house and drinking heavily. His sister took him in and he slept on the couch of the family's council house in Verona Avenue, Burnley.

She said later, "He cooked for himself and we hardly knew he was there. John wasn't stupid, he had a good head on him but he had been troubled with his nerves since his mother died."

In fact Smith had murder in mind. His ambition? To be Britain's most notorious assassin.

Little did his sister know, but hidden beneath the floorboards of her Burnley home was a document that would later leave top legal, government and police bosses reeling. It was a hit list. And the names on his chilling catalogue of execution targets were all top lawmen, all respected in their fields.

First to die was to have been the Lord Chancellor, Lord Hailsham. But Smith gave him a last-minute reprieve. Next were the northern judges William Openshaw and Phillip Kershaw – two men he blamed for his miserable time behind bars. Judge Kershaw had once jailed him for two and a half years. Finally would come Sir David McNee , as Metropolitan Commissioner, figurehead of the group he hated most – the police. The Home Secretary, William Whitelaw, was left out. His policies on prison reform made him a 'fair man' in Smith's eyes; he agreed with the 'short, sharp shock treatment' he had introduced. He also considered an attack on the Royal Family, but they were too closely guarded.

Smith's twisted need for vengeance was growing more calculated by the day. And of all the lawmen he grew to hate, it was the one who put him behind bars in the first place who topped the list: William Openshaw. Then came the final straw.

On May 11, 1981, Smith heard that his nephew had been sent to Borstal for

burglary. His sister Brenda told, "John came home, asked how Wayne had gone on and then said, 'Oh well, I suppose he'll learn the hard way'. Then he went out again. He just said, 'See you Bren' and that was the last I saw of him."

Hours later, Smith boarded a train to Preston. He was seen later that day waving his arms and screaming obscenities outside the town's crown court. The next day, Preston was in shock.

'Stabbed to death' screamed the headline in the *Lancashire Evening Post* on May 12. It read, "A murder hunt was launched today after Lancashire Judge William Openshaw was stabbed to death at his Preston home. It is thought the 68-year-old crown court judge grappled with an intruder in the driveway of his home Park House, in Garstang Road, Broughton."

The eminent judge had been found severely bleeding by his wife Joyce. By the time the ambulance arrived it was too late to save him. Police initially thought Judge Openshaw had disturbed a man trying to steal his car at breakfast time. The sinister truth was yet to come out. Police and detectives from all over Lancashire were drafted in to hunt a man – said to be heavily bloodstained – seen running from the house shortly before 9am.

The judge's large and leafy home, set back from the road and screened by trees, was sealed off by police. It was set directly opposite Broughton Police Station and officers guarded the entrance to the house's long drive. Lord Hailsham – at this time unaware of his lucky escape or his position on the hit list – was stunned by the tragedy and sent condolences.

Meanwhile, dog handlers and mounted police were brought in to comb parkland at the rear of the judge's home just off the main A6 Preston to Lancaster Road. Task force, regional crime squads and local detectives were called in. Local residents wept openly as Judge Openshaw's body, covered

Forensic experts in Broughton.

in a blanket, was taken away in a hearse. The vicar of St John the Baptist Church in Broughton visited the house to comfort a devastated Mrs Openshaw.

As the community reacted with horror, behind the scenes Mrs Openshaw was telling police how she came face-to-face with her husband's killer. She gave a full description of the man. She had explained that her husband had gone into the garage at around 8.30am. Minutes later she heard a voice.

Rushing in, she saw a man in the driving seat of her husband's green Ford Escort and became alarmed when she couldn't see her husband. She phoned police then returned to the garage where she saw her husband lying on the ground, covered in blood. She described her husband's killer as having a dark complexion, as being aged 20 to 40, with reasonably well-trimmed dark hair.

As Mrs Openshaw relived the terrible last moments of her husband's life, his colleagues mourned a dear friend. As a mark of respect the courts were closed. Judge Openshaw had been midway through a trial at the Sessions House on the day of his death. In Blackpool Crown Court, a minute's silence was observed before a trial began. And the tributes poured in from the great and the good.

Heather Steele was a barrister who occasionally sat in as deputy judge at crown court. She told the *Evening Post*, "I was a very great admirer of Bill Openshaw. He was a very kind man and a very fair man." Mr Roy Fisher, then High Sheriff of Lancashire and a personal friend of Judge Openshaw for 20 years, said, "It is tragic that a man who served law and good order for so long should die this way."

> **❝ He was a very kind man and a very fair man. ❞**

Mayor of Preston, Coun Ted Butcher, also weighed in with his tributes, saying, "I am extremely shocked to hear of the death of Judge Openshaw earlier today. Not only is it untimely but saddening because of the manner of his death. He was appointed recorder of Preston in 1958, and since that time I have known from my own personal experience and from what others who went before have told me, that he has given outstanding service not only on the bench but also in his civic capacity. To say that he will be sorely missed is a gross understatement. He and his family have been Prestonians in the fullest sense of the word and have always had Preston's interests at heart, and this has shone through in everything which Judge Openshaw did. The loss which his family has suffered is most tragic and our hearts go out to them and I know that they realise that the town's loss is also incalculable."

The entire town was reeling and none more so than its legal and political circles. Preston's then MP, Robert Atkins, said he was "sickened", and went on to pay tribute to Judge Openshaw's unrivalled knowledge of Preston North End. Hundreds more condolences flooded in, swamping the newsdesk at the *Lancashire Evening Post* where reporters struggled to take in the tide of grief and goodwill. But while the outpourings of grief continued, the police were on the trail of a killer.

John Smith is led away.

A new day and a new headline. 'Judge's killing: man held' said the *Lancashire Evening Post* on May 13. The news that a Lancashire man was being held in connection with the murder spread like wildfire throughout Preston. It was John Smith. But he wasn't in Preston – rather mysteriously he was in Scotland. In fact Smith, of Worsthorne, near Burnley, was being held by Scottish Police. Lancashire Police announced it would apply for a warrant to arrest him and detectives travelled to the border town of Hawick.

But he had not been arrested or charged in connection with the murder.

Up in Scotland, Smith appeared before court in Jedburgh charged with abduction, theft, assault and robbery. He was led into court with a blanket covering his head. These crimes, it emerged, had occurred in Scotland. So what had happened? What about a charge of murder? The people of Preston waited desperately for news.

But with the newspaper legally restricted from saying any more, the people of Preston had to watch and wait to see if justice was to be done. Meanwhile, Judge Openshaw's family faced the terrible task of officially identifying him, in order for the inquest could go ahead. To save his mother more heartbreak, Mr Openshaw's son, barrister Peter Openshaw, gave evidence of identification at the morning hearing at Preston's Coroner Court. He revealed his father had suffered a stroke ten years previously, but had made a good recovery and at the time of his death had been a well man for his age. The inquest was adjourned by deputy county coroner Michael Dolphin.

Then on May 14, came a breakthrough. "Man charged with Judge's murder" was the headline with the news that Smith had appeared briefly during a 12-minute hearing in court in Preston to hear the charges that had been levelled against him. During the hearing, Inspector William Duncan outlined the circumstances surrounding the charge and said a report would be sent to the director of public prosecutions as quickly as possible.

When asked to confirm his address as Verona Avenue, Worsthorne, Smith at first said 'yes', then shook his head and said 'no'. His solicitor Mr Barrington-Black explained his client was of no fixed abode. It was not to be the last time Smith tried to confuse the system. No attempt was made to apply for bail before the trial. He was remanded into custody for one week to Risley remand centre.

Just a day later, the inquest resumed and the true macabre nature of the judge's death came out for the first time. The 68-year-old had died of multiple stab wounds, the inquest heard. Dr Gordon Benstead, pathologist, said the senior circuit judge died from internal bleeding, caused by stab wounds to the head, back and chest. Coroner Mr Dolphin said he could now sign the appropriate forms to allow the inquest formalities to be completed. He closed the hearing.

With the inquest over, relatives were finally able to bury the civic leader. Emotions ran high for one of the biggest funerals seen in Lancashire for years. Leading public figures joined family and friends to pay their last respects. Around 30 top northern judges, three bishops, hundreds of civic leaders and many ordinary people attended the simple service at St Wilfred's Parish Church in picturesque Ribble Valley village, Ribchester, where the family had a home.

Preston's Crown Courts – scene of Judge Openshaw's recent cases – were closed as a mark of respect and so that staff could go to the burial service. At Preston Magistrates Court, a brief silence was observed. The small cortege, a hearse and two limousines flanked by police outriders, left the Judge's home in Garstang Road at 11.20 am. The cars carried widow Joyce Openshaw, 65, and other close relatives. Almost 30 minutes later the dignified procession drew up outside the 760-year-old parish church on the banks of the Ribble. It was clear this was no ordinary funeral.

The tiny village had a heavy police presence because leading public figures were attending, including including Mrs Justice Rose Heilbron, the judge in the infamous 'Mr Asia' trial. Police officers along the route stood to attention as the cortege passed and saluted with the strong contingent of ex-servicemen lowering their colours. Around 400 mourners packed into the church, with the service relayed to the many hundreds of others waiting outside.

They heard Rector of Ribchester, Canon John Cave, and Vicar of Broughton, the Rev Gerald Armstrong, lead the congregation in eulogies and prayers. Rector of Preston, Dr Michael Higgins, gave the address, paying tribute to the 'immense courage' of his family. He described the judge as a 'rare man' who was both respected and loved.

"It is very easy to see why Bill Openshaw was held in such respect. As a judge he was always scrupulously fair and his judgements were like the man – filled with good, down to earth, common sense. He was respected as a judge, as a man and for his community work," said Dr

The murder scene.

Higgins. "He had a good, warm relationship with everyone he came into contact with, from the highest to the lowest. And there was that famous, dry, droll, sense of humour that was so endearing."

After the traditional service, Judge Openshaw's body was committed to the family grave beside his parents Sir James and Lady Openshaw, and his sister Molly. Hundreds of dignitaries attended, including representatives from the council, church and police, as well as Tom Finney, club president from Judge Openshaw's beloved Preston North End. Then, in November 1981, with the town barely coming to terms with its collective grief, the murder trial began. "Knifeman's revenge on judge – QC," went the headline, as the horrific details of Smith's campaign of hate emerged for the first time.

The trial proved dramatic from the start. Smith, full of hatred and determined to buck the system in whatever way he could, delayed proceedings by refusing to recognise the court. In an outburst, he complained he was unable to get a fair trial and volunteered to sit in the cells throughout the hearing. "If I will get a fair and impartial hearing, I will take part in it," he shouted. "But I can't."

Earlier, Smith had turned his back on Mr Justice Lawson and sat out of sight on the floor of the dock. The judge shouted, "Will you turn round, I am speaking to you." Smith was spun round by two of the prison officers flanking him in the dock. As they held him tightly by the arms he cried out at the judge, "Are you satisfied now? You have to humiliate and degrade people, you sadist."

Mr Justice Lawson told him, "If you wish to go down to the cells you can, but it is not in your interests." Smith replied, "I don't recognise any court in this country," and was led down the steps into the cells by four prison officers.

Opening the case for the Crown, Mr Michael Maguire described in detail the 'disgraceful and unhappy' incidents of May 12 as Smith's sister Brenda sat sobbing in the public gallery above the court. The chilling facts of Smith's campaign were laid out for all to see.

Openshaw W.H. – Park House, Broughton. The entry in the phone book was like an open invitation to a grudge killer like Smith. The day before the murder, Smith had found the address of the judge and, armed with a hunting knife, boarded the Preston-bound train at Burnley. "He was full of hate, bent upon revenge, attempting to settle what he considered to be an old score," said Mr Maguire. "A long time ago, Judge Openshaw had sentenced the defendant to Borstal training. That is the motive for this murder."

He explained that Smith had walked from Preston station to the village of Broughton and waited for the judge's family to go to bed. He then sneaked into the back of the garage at the back of the house and hid in the rafters. "He waited hour after hour for an opportunity to exact retribution for that sentence of Borstal training, given to him long ago," said Mr Maguire. "In fact, he was somewhat impatient that the judge should keep him waiting so long."

But at 8.30am the judge had walked into the garage, wholly unsuspecting of the horrors that awaited him. Smith dropped from the rafters in front of him and stabbed him once in the body, shouting, "Now then, I've got you." The judge fell to the ground and raised his left arm in self-defence, but it was no use.

The judge would not have recognised his attacker as he fought to fend off the savage knife blows – their first meeting had hardly been memorable. But the much-loved judge had died a bloody death at the hands of a man bent on revenge. Smith had stabbed him 12 times in the head, neck and chest. As Judge Openshaw fought to hang on to life, Smith had attempted to start his car to escape, but was disturbed by Mrs Openshaw who heard a noise.

As soon as she saw Smith she ran into the house to call the police, unaware her husband lay dying on the floor. The murderer fled on foot, jumping a fence, running across a field and on to a nearby road where he flagged down a local businessman.

But while he made his escape, police had arrived at the house and found Judge Openshaw alive but unconscious. Inspector Peter Greenough was the first policeman on the scene. He told the court how he walked into the garage and spotted his body lying in front of his T-registered Ford Escort saloon. "He was lying on his stomach with his head slightly to the left side. I could see he was bleeding very heavily. He was gasping for breath, but unconscious."

Police officers desperately attempted to save his life by administering first aid, laying him on his side to assist his breathing and cutting away his clothing. An ambulance arrived in minutes but it was too late: tragically the judge was dead.

As Judge Openshaw lost his desperate battle for life, another man's ordeal was just beginning. As news of the crime and a description of the killer was flashed to every police force in Britain, Walter Hide, a company director from Goosnargh, near Preston, was driving to work. He was horrified when the heavily bloodstained Smith leapt into his passenger seat as he queued at the Broughton traffic lights in his green Austin Maxi. Much to Mr Hide's horror, the wild-eyed Smith pulled out a large knife from his waist and brandished it at the left side of his body.

"Just do as I say and you won't get hurt," he told him. Smith, who Mr Hide described as being in an agitated state, added, "I don't suppose you've been hi-jacked before."

That was the beginning of Mr Hide's six-hour ordeal. He was then forced to drive at speeds of around 60mph toward the Trough of Bowland, at which point Smith told him, "The guy had it coming to him. About 13 years ago he sent me down to Borstal."

At Burton, Mr Hide pulled in at a service station for petrol where Smith grabbed a blue turtle neck sweater lying in the back of the car, spat on the back of his hand and rubbed it on the material. Then he used it to cover the knife and got out of the car. He stood behind Mr Hide as he filled the petrol tank and paid at the kiosk for 20 cigarettes for Smith.

Back on the road Smith ordered the driver to go through any roadblocks that may have been erected on the motorway. The men then discussed how Smith could leave his captive. "He said he would have to tie me up in some trees. I tried to talk him out of this and made a suggestion that he could leave me somewhere, and I would give him half an hour to escape," said Mr Hide in a statement.

As the pair drove further into Scotland, Smith ordered Hide to stop the car at a wood near Hawick. After they both got out Smith handed Mr Hide the knife to cut up a set of jump leads. Mr Hide was then tied by his ankles and his wrists to the tree trunk with the wire.

Before leaving, Smith muttered perversely, "It's a bad thing to kill anyone." Mr Hide realised his life had been spared. He said, "Throughout this ordeal I tried to remain as calm as possible. I realised when he took me into the thicket I was in grave danger. That was the point of no return."

As Smith made off in his car, Mr Hide managed to struggle free of his bonds and ran to call the police. The officers of the Lothian and Borders police were quick to set up roadblocks, and eventually the car was spotted near the historic town of Jedburgh.

Forester Adam Wilson, 58, was working on Lord Lothin's estate when he watched the police cars swoop. "It was like a scene from Z-Cars," he later recalled. "One police car overtook the Maxi and one stayed behind. They wedged the car between their bumpers and forced him to stop. The driver made a run for it. He climbed over a fence and made off across a field. Three officers chased him and about 100 yards across a field they rugby tackled him."

The officers later told how they chased and disarmed the killer. PCs James Wilson, 32, and Gordon Smith, 21, said they followed the stolen car at speeds of up to 80mph and watched as Smith overtook traffic on dangerous corners. Two more officers, PCs Colin Nicholl, 36, and Malcolm Henderson, 31, manned a roadblock ahead, but one had to jump clear when Smith drove straight in to a checkpoint.

Eventually, after forcing Smith off the road, policemen Wilson, Nicholl and Smith chased him across a field and barged him to the ground. The knife was removed from his belt as two officers knelt on him. It had taken police just six hours to net the killer, but for victim Mr Hide it had seemed a terrifying eternity.

Smith later made a statement, and confessed to all three charges he faced – murder, kidnapping and false imprisonment. "The defendant's sole motive was revenge," said Mr Maguire to the court. "He planned to kill him, he intended to kill him and did in fact kill him in the savage manner I have described." Smith was found guilty of all charges.

A jury of seven men and five women took two and a half hours to reach a verdict on the murder charge by a 10:2 majority. They were unanimous in finding Smith guilty of a second charge of kidnapping businessman Mr Hide. Earlier Justice Lawson had told them there was no evidence to show Smith had been suffering from any mental disorder at the time of the killing. He also told them to ignore Smith's courtroom antics, including sitting cross-legged on the floor and shouting.

When the jury foreman delivered the guilty verdict, Smith just smiled calmly and looked up at his sister in the public gallery. Mr Justice Lawson then refused to allow Smith's counsel, Mrs Louise Godfrey, to read a statement which police had found hidden beneath floorboards at a house in Burnley. In it were details of plans to kill Judge Openshaw and his hit list of other targets.

Smith reacted angrily, "That document was written before I did this. I would like people to know." Then he told the judge, "I don't answer to you mister, or anyone else on this earth. I just let God Almighty judge me." He was then sentenced to life in prison.

> **❝ I just let God Almighty judge me. ❞**

As he started his long sentence, he knew he could very well end his days behind bars. But the cold-blooded killer said he had no regrets. He snarled defiantly as he was sent down, "I'd do exactly the same tomorrow. I'm not sorry for what I've done."

And as Mr Justice Lawson recommended he serve at least 25 years, he spat back, "I won't forget you. If I ever get out, I'll cut your throat." And he added, "I knew I would get caught. I knew I would end up rotting in jail. What have I to look forward to, spending the rest of my life inside? Still, it was worth it."

Justice Lawson told him, "You are a dangerous man and will remain so for some time."

Smith described himself as a 'monster' to police. But it was Judge Openshaw he blamed for that. "Why did he have to send me down in '68? If he hadn't he probably would still be alive and I wouldn't be the monster I am. Anyone who can kill anyone in cold blood is a monster, at least that's what people say."

Until the end of the trial Smith had insisted it was unfair, claiming he could get no justice in Britain, having killed a senior member of the bar. He wanted the case tried by the Court of European Rights, which was dismissed as 'nonsense' by Justice Lawson.

But Smith said in a statement, "How can I get a fair and impartial hearing when nearly everyone associated with the crown court system either knew this man or had friends that did? The only winners are the Police. Both me and Openshaw are the losers. I don't really know who is luckier, him or myself as I will be incarcerated for the rest of my life."

So Smith was jailed for life – and the Openshaw family was left with the terrible legacy of his tragic obsession. The wicked crime was, for them, a life sentence too.

The late Judge William Openshaw.

But as the portraits of the great Openshaw judges Sir James and William gaze down on Preston Crown Court to this very day – and with William's son Peter, the Hon Mr Justice Openshaw, and his wife Justice Caroline Swift following in the family trade as respected judges – it will be a long time before the legacy and service of the great Openshaw family is gone.

It will certainly never be forgotten.

CHAPTER FIVE

Death of an innocent

Imraan Vohra, Preston, July 11, 1985

PRESTON in the 1980s and two decades have passed since the first wave of immigrants began to arrive in the industrial town. Many came from India in the 1960s, lured by the promise of work in Lancashire's textile industries with the hope of better pay and a better standard of life for themselves and their families.

In the years that followed, more and more people came as the cotton mills continued to boom, slowly building their own communities in working class parts of the town and playing a prominent part in day-to-day life.

But with the decline of King Cotton and the consequent economic hardships, members of the Asian community joined their white counterparts in the dole queues. The work may have dried up but Preston was now very much home. Many became active in commercial quarters, setting up businesses and becoming respected and settled members of both their own communities and those of the existing white population. As a whole, the different communities rubbed along together well and peaceably, and Preston boasted an exemplary record of race relations.

The town was held up as a shining light, a beacon of hope and an example to those towns and cities struggling to cope with racial and cultural changes. But at the heart of the harmony lay an anomaly that was about to become all too apparent. Despite thousands of Asian people living in the town – largely Muslims from the Gujarati area of India – little effort was made to fully integrate the two communities by either side of the equation. It would take a town pulled together by a terrible tragedy to highlight the gulf in understanding and make the first steps toward stronger community ties and co-operation.

July 1985. The sun was shining and little nine-year-old Imraan Vohra was looking forward to the long summer that stretched ahead. The smiling youngster, who had two sisters and one brother, had just enjoyed a school trip to Bolton Abbey in

Yorkshire, where he had enjoyed japes with friends and schoolmates from Frenchwood Junior School. His younger brother and sister, Taheir and Hafeeza, were also pupils at the school. A photograph taken that day would show him confident and happy, posing in the midst of his school friends and smiling straight into the camera. Bright and diligent, football-loving Imraan was a young boy with a busy routine.

From 9am to 3.30pm during term-time, Imraan took his place in the classroom with other boys and girls. But unlike many of his classmates, Imraan's education did not end at the final bell. For two and half hours every weeknight, he and other Muslim children took extra religious studies at the mosque in Clarendon Street, one of five Islamic centres in Preston. There they would be taught the principal tenets of their faith, learning passages from the Koran by heart to adopt a heritage stretching back 1,400 years and thousands of miles. After studies, Imraan would head home to the family house in James Street, one of the oldest areas of Preston, where his family lived in harmony alongside other cultures. At the time, there were 270 Asian families living in the Frenchwood area.

Imraan was a competent student, and he had a real talent with his hands. He had just made a 3D coloured mosque out of cardboard during the Eid festival at the end of Ramadan. He loved football and sport in general, and had just collected certificates for sprinting, the high jump and obstacle racing in that year's sports day.

Imraan was well-behaved and full of youthful exuberance, particularly close to his class teacher James Vaney. The teachers valued his maturity and sense of humour, which made him stand out from other pupils. Headteacher, Elaine Cowell, later told the *Lancashire Evening Post*, "His delightful sense of humour set him apart because you could joke with him in a mature way. His classmates wanted and sought his friendship because of his happy and sensible nature."

His written English was flawless for his age, his school exercise book typical of the innocence and willingness to learn of any nine-year-old boy. In the latest exercise, he wrote about animals:

> *The donkey is a stubborn animal with very long ears. The kangaroo has strong hind legs which enable him to move forward in great leaps. A bear has a shaggy coat and strong claws. It can hug a person to death.*

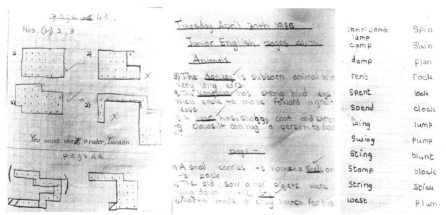

Imraan's school work.

In a chilling portent, the word "death" was to be his last written entry.

July 11, 1985, dawned a drizzly, changeable day and as school finishing time beckoned, the weather brightened up with intermittent periods of sunshine, with temperatures reaching 68°F. In nearby Avenham Park, youngsters played hip-hop music on the bandstand in their T-shirts, soaking up the early evening rays. Imraan left school as usual at 3.30pm after a brief game of marbles with his friends.

Then he disappeared.

At first his anxious parents Ismail and Habiba Vohra thought he may have been distracted with a playmate on his way home – out of character but not impossible. But as the minutes and the hours ticked by, it was clear something was very wrong. At 9pm, frantic with worry, they reported their son missing to police.

"Alert as boy, 9, goes missing," rang out the headline of the *Lancashire Evening Post* story the next day, urging the public to report any sightings of the little boy. A major search was launched by Lancashire Police. First his known play areas were targeted and mounted police and dog handlers were deployed to scour Avenham Park and Miller Park. As Imraan's parents watched and wept with fear, an underwater search team prepared to search the River Ribble which borders the parks.

Superintendent John Hilton co-ordinated the search, saying on July 12, "It is very unusual for this boy not to have returned home from school last night. We have checked all the boy's relatives and are now searching areas where he is known to play. We believe he had several 'dens' in the parks. Obviously we are very concerned for his safety."

But just two days later, on July 13, the very worst of news was heard. "Missing boy found dead," tolled the front-page headline of the *Evening Post*. At 5am that morning, a terrible find had been made in Avenham Park. Following a combined search by mounted police and more than 150 volunteers from the Asian community, the small boy's body was found by two search members on the park near the Frenchwood recreation ground.

But as the *Evening Post* went to press on that terrible morning, police were issuing few details about the circumstances of the horrifying discovery. The full reality about the sadistic death of a nine-year-old boy was yet to be revealed. And when it was, it would leave a community shattered.

A press conference was scheduled for that day. The grim details, when they emerged, left Preston in shock. Young Imraan's near naked body was partially hidden under a bush. When two of the search party found him, he was lying face up in undergrowth, 100 yards from the Old Tram Bridge near an area known locally as 'The 49 Steps'.

Imraan was naked apart from a shirt. His trousers, underwear, shoes and jacket were found scattered nearby. He had been sexually assaulted and then strangled to death. Detective Superintendent John Boyd, who was leading the investigation, announced the chilling details of the death of the

❝ He had been sexually assaulted and then strangled to death. ❞

youngster, adding, "We need help in filling the mystery hours after he left school because we are reasonably certain he was killed on Thursday."

Immediately a massive police manhunt swung into action. As Imraan's family grieved and residents struggled to come to terms with the discovery, 60 officers were put on the case. On July 15, police issued a stark warning – there was no guarantee the killer would not strike again. The murder enquiry rapidly became a race against time.

Officers desperately followed up every lead as schoolteachers across the town urged pupils to take extra care on their way home. Terrified parents escorted or drove their children to school and activities, fearful of leaving them alone and vulnerable. Members of the frightened local community demanded police give them more protection.

Det Supt Boyd told the *Post*, "Anybody who attacks a nine-year-old boy, sexually assaults him and strangles him, cannot be normal. You cannot get any worse than this crime. It cannot be ruled out that he will strike again."

Police revealed that Imraan's body had few marks of violence upon it, apart from the strangulation caused by an unknown ligature. They also believed the youngster had gone to the park on his own, probably enticed there by his attacker. Police were convinced he could have known his killer.

In a desperate bid to encourage witnesses who may have seen Imraan on his ill-fated journey, police released a picture of a brown, beige and red anorak similar to the one Imraan was wearing, hoping against hope it would jog someone's memory.

Meanwhile, the appalling grief at the killing of young Imraan brought residents of all races closer together. The shock and disgust at the murder of an innocent child was universal. Preston Community Relations Officer, Farouk Desai, told the *Evening Post*, "People from all cultures and races are offering help to the family and police. White people volunteered alongside Asians in the search for one of the area's children. It's a small parish and a big family and this has struck people very hard."

The weekend after Imraan's murder, Mr Desai spent long hours working with community leaders to comfort Imraan's father, Ismail Vohra, who was described as a strong-willed man who was "shouldering the burden of grief felt by his family." He said hundreds of people were expected to attend Imraan's funeral, due to be held at Preston Cemetery. "Everybody just wants to share the grief," said Mr Desai.

At Imraan's school, work had to continue as usual as teachers and pupils reeled from the horror. Elaine Cowell told the *Lancashire Evening Post*, "Each one of us on the staff feels as if we have had a personal loss. Every child at the school becomes a part of their lives while they are here." She said the shock had barely subsided: "We were all numbed from disbelief at first, it probably protected us from some of the pain. But now reality has set in. You have to concentrate on achieving normality in your surroundings."

The murder scene taped off by police in Avenham Park.

In the first of a number of heartbreaking appeals, Imraan's father Ismail pleaded with his son's killer to come forward. During a press conference he fought back tears, telling the assembled reporters that Imraan was a "good boy" who had never done anything wrong and knew perfectly well not to go off with strangers:

"I have no idea who might have done this. I hope the community will help the police arrest whoever did it. I have lost my son and I don't want it to happen to anybody else."

Other community leaders reached out to residents, asking anybody with information to come forward to police. Oman Munshi, one of the leaders of Preston Muslim Society and a family friend of the Vohras, said, "It is important this man is found. The sooner he is caught the better it is for everyone. We have distributed a leaflet into the community and we are asking the members of our society to help the police all they can. I have no why idea this thing happened. Everyone is completely shattered. He was a very popular little boy and everyone is doing their best to comfort his family."

To reach out to as many people as possible, posters appealing for help were issued by leaders of Clarendon Street mosque in both English and Gujarati. Police also attended the daily prayer meetings at the mosque, interviewing worshippers and trying to piece together information.

Murder Hunt.

On behalf of the society we make this sincere plea to all residents in the area to assist the police in their investigation to find the murderer of the innocent boy Imraan Vohra.
We request all our members to co-operate fully with the police department in every possible way. If you think you have any information, no matter how trivial it may seem, please tell the police.
Your cooperation is greatly appreciated.

Thank you.

As well as the poster appeal, loudspeaker vans were deployed to broadcast appeals for help in both Gujarati and English. The first major lead was sparked when a witness described seeing two men, one Asian, one white. The Asian man, suspected of meeting Imraan outside his school on the afternoon he disappeared, was described as being in his late twenties, 5ft 10ins tall, slim with straight black collar-length hair parted on the left side, and wearing black trousers. He was seen in Frenchwood Knoll, opposite the junior school gate.

The white man was spotted with an Asian boy similar to Imraan in appearance a week earlier in Miller Park on Thursday July 4. He was aged 35-40, 5ft 10ins, broad and muscular with a "square, puffy face" and fair complexion. He had thick mousey hair covering his ears and was wearing light coloured upper clothing and dark trousers. One witness suggested he may have had a light brown, medium-sized, smooth coated dog with him. The Asian boy accompanying him was "aged about ten years" and wore light blue trousers.

Artist impressions of the pair were issued, but to no avail. Police admitted they were disappointed with the "lukewarm" response, receiving less than a dozen calls. They took further action, getting Gujarati captions printed under the artist's impressions and handing them out on leaflets to the Asian community at prayer meetings and pinning them to notice boards at doctor's surgeries and libraries. By mid-August, with a limited response to the enquiry, it was clear the murder team needed more help. They turned to the BBC's *Crimewatch*, which agreed to re-enact Imraan's final hour in the hope it provoked a response from the programme's 13 million viewers.

"Can TV help catch a killer?" asked the *Post* headline as TV bosses used a look-a-like schoolboy to reconstruct the dramatic moment the young boy was lured to his death. Twenty of Imraan's schoolmates interrupted their summer holidays to re-enact the events of the last day he was seen alive. Friends and neighbours who helped look for him when he disappeared joined Lancashire Constabulary's mounted branch and dog section to re-stage the search.

Crimewatch bosses decided to take a risk, acting on the witness tip-off that Imraan may have left school with a young man who called out to him as he left the front gates. They dramatised what could have happened, filming the schoolboy actor dressed identically to Imraan being confronted and walking off with the sinister figure, praying the gamble would pay off. Was he Imraan's killer? Presented by Nick Ross and Sue Cook, the programme was aired at 9.25pm on August 29, while detectives in Lancashire manned the first floor incident room overnight, waiting for a call that could mark a breakthrough in the case. Det Supt Boyd appeared on the show making an emotive plea for information. Despite the theme of the dramatisation, he explained detectives still had three main categories of killer in mind.

Scenes from a reconstruction screened by BBC's *Crimewatch*.

One: that he was known to Imraan and he accompanied him to the park willingly. Two: It was a predatory park homosexual who lost his temper when the boy would not submit. Three: That it was a travelling opportunist sex attacker.

But most officers favoured the first choice. The police received hundreds of calls that night and followed up 25 new lines of enquiry, but none was the call that was so badly needed. The killer still eluded capture and neither of the two men was ever identified.

❝ The killer still eluded capture and neither of the two men was ever identified. ❞

Ismail Vohra buried his nine-year-old son still not knowing why he had died. The pain and confusion was clear on his face as he stood in a sodden Preston cemetery seven weeks after the death of his innocent young boy. At times he seemed totally bewildered by the proceedings, as if trying to work out why he was there, to confront the inexplicable horror of Imraan's death. As prayers were said at the graveside, Mr Vohra's eyes stared blankly over the scene with the rain bucketing down, his hands – caked in mud from Imraan's plot – covering his face as he sought private solace.

Around the grave at the rear of the cemetery stood hundreds of fellow Muslims. Some came from as far as London and Yorkshire, others from the close-knit Preston community had taken time off work or closed their businesses to attend the funeral. Side-by-side, sharing grief, were neighbours from the Frenchwood area, teachers and classmates from Imraan's school, policemen and local councillors. All thoughts were with Imraan and his family as the simple service was conducted through a loudspeaker to reach those furthest from the graveside.

Imraan's last journey had begun from his home in James Street, where the simple teak coffin was carried into the back of a red van by relatives. According to the traditions of the Muslim faith, only men are allowed at funerals. So the men set off in convoy for the cemetery while the women, including Imraan's mother Habiba, stayed at home.

Inside the graveyard, mourners removed their shoes, faced east and stood on plastic sheets to join in prayers led by Ibrahim Ali from the Preston Muslim Society. Imraan's coffin lay by a pile of stones and discarded shoes, with umbrellas, religious caps and waterproofs covering those on the makeshift prayer mat.

With the opening ceremony over, it was left to his father and relatives to carry Imraan a short distance to the gated Muslim plot where he was buried. At his graveside lay messages and cards,

Mourners line up alongside Imraan's grave.

including a sealed message from the police team trying to catch his killer. The message, attached to the wreath, was from Det Supt Boyd and other officers who had vowed to seek justice for little Imraan. Mr Vohra did not cry but his grief could not be mistaken. Following the heightened emotions of the funeral, the police hoped more leads would surface but, in reality, the investigation was going nowhere fast. Police now feared they had encountered a wall of silence in a frightened community. The leads were petering out.

In desperation, the *Lancashire Evening Post*, the Muslim Society and Preston Council put up a total of £4,000 reward money for information leading to the killer's arrest. But still nothing.

Det Supt Boyd voiced his fears that at least one member of the community knew something and that he and his team of detectives had interviewed him or her. He explained, "It may well be that somebody has been asked to tell the police a lie in relation to a dear one and dear one's movements. They might not fully realise the implications behind this, and they might be protecting the killer in the mistaken belief they are being loyal. Obviously it is vital this person should consider their position."

He was convinced that Imraan knew his killer, later saying, "I am sure that Imraan would not go off with a total stranger. He would certainly not go off into the park with a stranger. It had to be someone he knew. Perhaps the killer strangled him after committing an indecent act because Imraan could identify him.

"Someone must be carrying a terrible burden. Maybe someone carrying that burden had since confided in somebody else. I would like somebody who left the area without good reason to contact us in strictest confidence."

By now Det Supt Boyd's team had been working 11 hours a day for nine weeks. He paid tribute to their dedication: "They have worked both hard and enthusiastically and the morale is still high despite the lack of results. They all feel that the next day could bring in the kind of initiative we so badly need. We have uncovered a number of possibilities over the weeks but our follow-up enquiries have always ended up eliminating them."

One of the team's most time-consuming tasks was trying to trace visitors to Avenham Park on the day of the murder, with more than 200 people remaining unidentified and just 35 traced. Despite co-operation from the park's homosexual community, many of the others remained untraced. Only a handful had contacted police, leaving officers frustrated with the pace of the investigation. Several suspects had been eliminated and an ID parade proved fruitless. But with little progress on the investigation, 15 of the 60 police officers assigned to the case were sent back to normal duties in divisions across the county. But Det Supt Boyd insisted the investigation was not being scaled down.

As the investigation stalled, Asian leaders moved quickly to stamp out rumours that their "closed rank" community had already meted out punishment to Imraan's murderer. A story picked up in legal circles in Preston suggested that the public shame of having a sex killer in their midst might be too much for the Muslim faith to bear. Instead of unmasking him through the law courts, they might lose less face by exiling the murderer to India.

But representatives of the ethnic minorities in the town were eager to dispel the suggestion before rumours caught hold. Police were equally keen to scotch the story, reminding the public that children of all races must be afforded extra protection with a child killer on the loose. Mr Munshi of the Muslim Society told the *Evening Post* that unilateral action on their part was "just not feasible," saying, "It would be quite out of character for Muslims to hide such horrible things. Quite the reverse in fact. We would want it out in the open.

"Naturally if the killer was a Muslim it would bring shame on us and harm our community, but that is not a strong enough reason to hide his identity." He added they would not consider deporting him back to India if they found him. "That would mean taking the law into our hands and we simply would not do that. It also couldn't happen without the elders finding out. It would be leaked and we would put a stop to it. We are a well disciplined people and we accept the police role in this."

His sentiments were echoed by Mr Desai: "It is important we put an end to this rumour; there is no substantiation to it at all. Local people want this killer brought to justice in the normal way."

But it seemed that not everybody in the Asian community had been as frank. Mr Desai explained that uncertainty was put into some people's minds earlier in the investigation when, rightly or wrongly, they were labelled illegal immigrants. He said, "I went to great lengths to explain all the rules and regulations governing this and whether some were covered by Government amnesty. People may have shut themselves away from police at the start but I don't think that's the case now. I may be wrong and the fear may be not have dispersed from their minds 100 per cent. I hope this is not holding anybody back."

Eleven weeks after Imraan's death, there was another day of pain for his family. On what should have been the youngster's tenth birthday, instead of the planned celebrations at the terraced home on cobbled James Street, the family offered prayers to Allah – asking for the murderer to be captured before he strikes again. Ismail Vohra told the *Evening Post*, "We are all still very shocked, my wife cannot believe it. The children miss their brother terribly. Imraan is always in my thoughts and it means everything to me that the killer is caught. The £4,000 reward posted by the *Evening Post* is a good idea and I really hope it helps the police."

After the family prayers, Ismail walked to the nearby mosque to give solitary prayers for his son.

Pupils at Imraan's school also remembered him on his birthday, before normal lessons started. Headteacher Elaine Cowell said, "We were aware that he would have been ten today and remembered him specifically for that."

Imraan Vohra.

Meanwhile, police marked what would have been Imraan's special day by issuing a photofit of a new witness seen running away from the scene of the murder. Described as a "frightened boy", he was spotted sprinting down South Meadow Lane away from the Avenham Park area at 4.15pm on July 11 – the approximate time and place of the killing. He was said to have a frightened expression and was running flat out.

They also revealed they were trying to locate an anonymous caller who rang in after the *Crimewatch* programme, claiming she was living with a man acting suspiciously on the day of Imraan's death. But she gave false identities for herself and her boyfriend. Det Supt Boyd said, "If this was a hoax it was certainly an elaborate one because she was on the phone quite some time."

It was now almost three months since the killing and police re-interviewed 230 former classmates of Imraan in an attempt to find fresh information. Detectives spent seven days at Frenchwood Primary School comparing statements made after the murder. The team tried to establish if the youngster had confided in friends about a secret meeting with a stranger. They also wanted to investigate a rumour that Imraan had an extra £5 in his pocket the day before his brutal death. But both lines of enquiry drew a blank. And information to the incident room at Preston police station had dried up.

The team had also investigated possible links to other child killings, including that of Jason Swift and Barry Lewis the year before in Essex and South London who were murdered by a paedophile ring. But they concluded Imraan's death was the work of an isolated killer. Det Supt Boyd said, "The public response which was excellent originally has dwindled to virtually nothing. We are not critical of this because the murder happened almost three months ago."

There was to be no breakthrough.

Five years after his son's death, Imraan Vohra told the *Evening Post* he still hoped the murderer would be brought to justice. The pain was visible in his eyes as he explained, in his broken English, how his heart had been broken:

"Why Imraan? Why us? I just don't know. I hurt inside. Little things remind me of what happened. Parents should keep their eyes on their children. I don't want other parents to go through what I, my wife and children have gone through. He would have been 15 in October; when I see groups of children his age I think about him. Since it happened we have tried to rebuild our lives but we will never forget Imraan."

He said he could not keep many pictures of his son on display as it was too upsetting, adding, "Someone should have been brought to justice." But there was to be no relief from the heartache for the Vohras.

In 1993, Mr Vohra offered out the hand of friendship to another family hit by tragedy. He wrote to the family of Akhlaq Razzaq, found dead in a park close to his Berkshire home. Despite the eight year gap there were chilling similarities between the killings. Both Asian, both nine, both found strangled and stripped in parkland close to their homes. As painful memories came flooding back, Imraan's father offered his sympathy to Akhlaq's parents and said he hoped this latest tragedy would cast fresh light on his own son's death. But no evidence, other than circumstantial, was ever to link the two brutal crimes.

A decade passed, then in 1991 – more than 16 years after Imraan's death – detectives announced the decision to launch a 'cold case' review into the murder. Using advancements in technology to re-screen evidence forensically, they hoped to open new avenues of investigation and were sure they could still catch the child killer. Det Supt Mick Turner, leading the inquiry team, said about a dozen key witnesses – many of them children at the time of the murder – would be re-interviewed by police hoping to discover fresh information. Door-to-door enquiries would also take place. But he admitted the police did not actually have any new leads. Det Supt Turner, who took part in the original search for Imraan as a junior officer, said, "His death remains at the forefront of the minds of his family and the community. We are currently reviewing certain aspects of the initial inquiry but I must stress there is no significant new information at this time."

He explained to the *Evening Post*, "People may have information they did not feel confident to give at the time. We are also speaking to scientists who were involved at the time to see if their discoveries have moved on. But we do not want to get everyone's hopes up by thinking we have a magic new piece of evidence. We don't.

"It is still important to everybody who was around in Preston at the time. We hope to bring some resolution for the family who have had to live with this for all these years. There are plenty of police officers who worked on it who are still working, myself included. We know that the community are behind us and nobody wants there to be a child killer walking free."

The Vohra family took heart from the new investigation, with Ismail taking part in a rare interview with the *Evening Post* and explaining how the crime still stole a little bit of happiness from his family every single day.

He reflected, "For 16 years our family has had to face up to the fact that no-one has been caught. It still affects us every day and none of the family has forgotten Imraan. It is very important to me that someone is caught for this. We are pleased the police are going to look at it again and we just hope it leads to someone being caught. We will be pleased if this leads to justice."

The family still live in James Street, the home to which their small son never returned, "We think about him with every day that passes. I still remember him as

The house in James Street, where the Vohra family still live.

the lovely son he was. He was popular and did well at school. His teacher at school always had good words for him. He was a good boy."

But by 2002 the review had so far yielded little and the 20-strong team of detectives moved on to the next phase – and then a revelation. A forensic team, led by renowned expert Dr John David, obtained a partial DNA profile of the killer for the first time. Detectives announced that more than 90 men would be DNA tested to see if they could find a match, ruling out rumours of a mass screening of the public.

Det Supt Turner explained, "Nine hundred pieces of possible evidence have been examined and DNA removed. As the next part of the inquiry we want to mouth-swab 90 members of the public. But these people are not necessarily suspects. The screening techniques are very sensitive; we have to rule out any possibilities that the evidence is contaminated. For instance, some of these people were members of the community who set up a search team for Imraan after he went missing; we have to rule everybody out to narrow it down, including family and friends."

Anybody who worked on the case, from police to forensic scientists, had to be eliminated, pushing the number of people to be tested to 200. Only half of those swabbed were to be Asian men. Around 14 people who died since the original inquiry posed a problem to the team – should they exhume their bodies? But this was ruled out. Instead post-mortem examination samples were used to cross check where possible.

Behavioural profilers and experts from the National Crime Faculty were drafted in to maximise information brought in through witnesses and forensic evidence. An eyewitness also came forward to provide a significant new lead. The woman, a young girl at the time of the murder, told police how she heard an Asian man call Imraan's name before leading him away on the day he disappeared.

Then for the first time, a breakthrough.

Detectives arrested a 40-year-old Asian man in London. He was taken to Preston police station where he underwent DNA tests. Police appealed for, and were given, an additional 48 hours to question the man. But the hopes were short-lived for Imraan's family. He was released without

❝ Detectives arrested a 40-year-old Asian man in London. ❞

charge – the police convinced he was not the boy's killer. The net was widened. More people were DNA tested and police liaised with other forces, convinced that Imraan's killer may have struck elsewhere. Evidential DNA from Imraan's murder was matched against that of unsolved crimes across the country, making use of the *Catchem* database of UK murders.

Detectives then decided to reconstruct Imraan's death for a second time. Again to be featured in a television appeal, this time on Granada TV's *Crimefile*. Members of the original search team made an emotional return to the scene of the murder, 17 years after they made their macabre discovery. Again, a boy actor was recruited to play Imraan, returning to the little boy's school haunts. For many the very real emotion re-surfaced as the heartbreaking details of the case were raked over.

Ahmed Bhayat, a 37-year-old from James Street – where Imraan lived – took part in the original search party that found the little boy's body. He told how the community had been heartbroken and scared following the discovery: "It was horrific. Other people with us were quite distraught at the time. We knew he used to play in dens so at first we thought he'd gone walking about and had hidden in a den, but as time went by we realised he couldn't stay out all night, the weather was terrible." Another member of the community who helped with the original search was Bashir Ahmed, 39, of Brixton Road. He told the *Post*, "It feels a bit weird coming back here because we've not been in this area of the park since then, but we'll do anything to catch the killer."

Elyas Asmal, 42, of Frenchwood Knoll, said, "It's our duty to help as much as we can. We'd all like to know who did it. Somebody must know something." *Crimefile* went on air and police were delighted with the response when two callers gave the same name to police. The tape of the reconstruction was distributed to another six Asian radio and television networks and they agreed to broadcast some in the UK, some in Asia. The hunt had gone worldwide.

Meanwhile, police officers were meticulously shifting through 200 potential DNA matches through the national databases, working through pages and pages of notes and witness statements and logging everything on the Home Office large major enquiry database Holmes. But despite their efforts, little new ground was

uncovered. Then in September 2002, came a blow to the investigation team. A massive child porn probe forced the team to vacate the incident room at Lancashire Police HQ at Hutton. But despite being sidelined, the Vohra team vowed to track Imraan's killer and made the difficult decision to finally reveal a key piece of evidence that they had kept to themselves for almost two decades.

"Trophy of Evil," shouted the chilling headline in the *Evening Post* on December 18. "Revealed: Chilling calling card of Imraan's deranged murderer."

Imraan's trousers were tied to a tree, possibly to alert officers to what was hidden in the foliage.

The story went on, "This is the sickening image of murdered schoolboy Imraan Vohra's trousers. They were ripped off the youngster's body and tied to a tree by the evil killer just 6ft from where Imraan lay."

THE 49 STEPS MURDER: A COMMUNITY IS LEFT IN DESPAIR — PAGE TWO.

DRAGNET FOR SEX KILLER

Police chief's plea

THE HUNT for the sex killer of a nine-year-old boy became a race against time today.

By CHRIS BIRDSALL and BOB WESTERDALE

Detectives investigating the murder of Imraan Vohra admitted: "There is no guarantee this man will not strike again."

Police were today desperately following up every lead as school head teachers warned youngsters to take extra care on their way home.

The popular Asian youngster was found strangled in undergrowth at Preston's Avenham Park at 8 am on Saturday. He had been missing since leaving Frenchwood Junior School on Thursday.

He was naked except for a shirt. His trousers, underwear, shoes and jacket were found nearby. He had been sexually assaulted.

Sixty officers, led by Det Supt John Boyd, second in command of Lancashire CID, immediately called on the Asian community to help track down the murderer.

Det Supt Boyd said: "Anybody who attacks a nine-year-old boy, sexually assaults him and strangles him, cannot be normal. You cannot get any worse than this crime.

"It cannot be ruled out that he will not strike again."

There were few marks of violence on the boy's body, apart from strangulation caused by an unknown binding. Police believe it was unlikely Imraan would have gone,

"And despite many theories on why the murderer left the disturbing trophy for all to see, he has never been caught. Today, detectives unveiled the dramatic new twist in the case as they step up their hunt for the deranged killer."

The sadistic twist to the story sent shockwaves reverberating through Preston and communities still recovering from the tragedy. The young boy had been strangled with his own trousers, before they were hung in the tree. Police had kept the information back hoping it would be the key to catch a killer. But now they had been forced to make a throw of the dice, in the hope it would jog a memory or shock a witness into coming forward. From this point onwards, they knew they would have to rely on DNA evidence to pin him down.

Criminal profilers and experts came up with a number of theories about why the killer ripped off the youngster's trousers and left them tied to the tree, almost 6ft above the ground. Some believed it was used as a calling card or trophy, personalising the murder.

Another theory was that the killer felt remorse and hung the trousers in the tree so the body would be found quickly. The area was fairly overgrown at the time and the trousers may have been out there to alert officers to what was hidden in the dense foliage. Similarly, the killer may have been sensitive to Imraan's cultural background. Islamic religion dictates that bodies should be buried as soon a possible, preferably within 24 hours. Friday is considered a Holy Day and so a good day to bury your dead. Imraan went missing on a Thursday but he wasn't found until Saturday.

Every time the story was featured in the *Evening Post*, police received a couple of new names to chase. But detectives were well aware they could be clutching at straws and hoped the startling new images would prompt new leads. They also took advantage of the publicity over the revelation to make a fresh appeal for a scruffy-looking, pot-bellied man seen in the park with a boy matching Imraan's description. Det Supt Turner told the *Evening Post*, "All we need is a name."

The new information prompted another TV appeal, this time on BBC's *Crimewatch*, 17 years after the programme first attempted to help. Thirty calls were made to the incident room with a dozen different names put forward as possible suspects. Finally one part of the jigsaw, the young man seen running in a panic from Avenham Park the day Imraan died, came forward and was eliminated from the enquiry using DNA.

Imraan's father, Ismail Vohra.

With new leads to follow and the enquiry team growing in confidence, the hunt for the killer went nationwide. Eight hundred men from across the UK, including some in their eighties, faced DNA tests in addition to the 200 swabbed already. The new DNA technology, known as SNIPS, was used to analyse samples in several different ways.

A team of retired detectives who worked on the original enquiry was also drafted in to help. This included Ron Hooper and Donald Biscomb, who remembered the case all too well. Former Detective Inspector Hooper, a sergeant on the original team who still lives in Preston, retired from the force eight years previously. He told the *Lancashire Evening Post*, "When it actually broke I was a detective sergeant and I recall I was on nights. We knew that this young boy was missing and I remember as I was going off duty that morning there were search teams coming into Preston police station at about five or six o'clock in the morning. I went home to bed to find the following day that they had found his body in Avenham Park and it was a murder inquiry."

Donald Biscomb, also from Preston, spent 31 years in the police and had been retired for eight years when the case reopened. He was a DCI at Preston at the time of the murder. He said, "I worked on the original murder inquiry and I was disappointed that the killer was never brought to justice. Although we did do a six-month, painstaking investigation at that time, we had no concrete evidence and DNA was only in its infancy. Now we have the advantage of a full DNA profile and I feel sure that we will get the person responsible.

"It was a shocking murder. It is particularly distressing when children are murdered."

In May 2003, top criminal profiler Karl Roberts, from Teesside University, spoke to the *Evening Post* exclusively about his profile of the sex beast. He told the reporter he was still likely to be living within the local community, saying, "He is an active paedophile. He may have lain low for a while, but this is somebody who is going to take the opportunity, when it's available, to approach children.

❝ He is an active paedophile. He may have lain low for a while... ❞

"This is somebody who has taken a bit of time about it, whose approach is befriending. He tends towards making a relationship of trust, this is the most likely way." Dr Roberts profiled the offender as a young man, of average intelligence with a low social status and low self-esteem. He said he may well have been sexually abused as a child: "At his youngest, he was in his late twenties at the time of the offence, possibly in his thirties or older. This is because of the maturity with which he has committed the offence.

"It has been done in a reasonable, self-controlled way, which you do not see in attacks by younger people."

The profile states he is of average intelligence. "We look at what evidence there is for complex planning. Really intelligent individuals tend to have the wildest sexual fantasies. Again, those at the opposite end of the spectrum tend to go for a more simplistic approach. This has got aspects of planning, aspects of sexual fantasy, but they are not really very complex.

"He has not got fantastically good social skills. I do not think this person is going to have a huge range of social friends at the time or since."

Dr Roberts painted a picture of a man who was not a loner, but did not have a wide social group; someone who focused on children because they were not threatening, finding it easy to talk to them and finding them preferable:

"He has probably not got a fantastically high status occupation – this is not somebody who has achieved educationally or socially. If he is employed it is not going to be high status; it's not going to be somebody like a teacher. His primary sexual interest is towards children, and male children in particular and that's something that is ongoing and possibly even previous to the crime. I think the offender at the time had got levels of local knowledge, that is often obtained from living and working in an area."

He explained, "Many offenders choose where they live to carry out these attacks because it is where they are most comfortable. Why would somebody offend like that if they had a flat, or access to something like that? There are various reasons – there may have been somebody living there that, at the time, rendered it difficult. He may have lived in an environment where someone could see."

He added that, although the offender had attacked in a public park, it was in an isolated spot: "If the person has previous convictions, a lot will be related to children in some way. Before the crime I think this person is going to have been around the area and has possibly even turned up with Imraan in the days or weeks prior to the murder. He may have befriended Imraan and gone with him.

"Anybody who knows the character at all may have seen behavioural changes since the offence, tied in with anxiety, stress, distress, sleep disturbance, irritability and social withdrawal. This is not a fantastically confident person – he is not going to pursue social relationships so much.

"I think the only time you would have seen the issue of murder raised is if the subject came up. All the recent coverage of the case may have heightened his anxiety. There may have been changes in his behaviour over the last few weeks."

Police reiterated the clue the profile gave. Det Insp Joe Kellett, of Preston CID, urged any other sex abuse victims to come forward in the hope of catching Imraan's killer. He said, "Dr Roberts is clearly indicating that the offender in this case is likely to have committed other sexual acts on young boys. We would like to hear from anyone who has knowledge of persons who, either before or since the murder of Imraan Vohra, has committed this type of offence.

"There may be victims out there who have been sexually abused who may not have reported it to the police previously. The offender might still be out there and it could be the same person that sexually assaulted and killed young Imraan."

The incident room.

The appeal hit home.
Five men came forward, saying they were victims of sex attacks in the 1980s – two at the time of the murder. One of the attacks showed disturbing similarities to Imraan's death. They started following up the cases, hoping against hope for a breakthrough. But with little to go on, the probe was scaled back.

❝ Five men came forward, saying they were victims of sex attacks in the 1980s... ❞

In 2008 Imraan Vohra would have been celebrating his 33rd birthday. He could have been married, had children, been successful professionally and made his mother and father proud. But instead, the loving, happy, well-mannered child became prey to a cowardly attacker who did not see the person he would become – instead he abused and disposed of the vibrant young boy for a moment's gratification.

A horrific crime that ripped apart not just a family, but a whole community and would echo through the decades, the horror never diminishing. Imraan's death is one of Lancashire's largest, most painstaking and high-profile unsolved cases, and detectives will never give up the hunt for the man who cut his life short in the most sadistic, inhumane of ways. Because somewhere, probably in the heart of Preston's peaceful, culturally diverse community, a perverted child killer could still be walking the streets, preying on the young and vulnerable.

And somebody probably knows who that killer is.

CHAPTER SIX

The vanishing

Helen McCourt, Billinge, February 9, 1988

WEATHER forecasters spent the day warning people not to venture outdoors unless it was absolutely necessary. Hurricane K was heading towards Britain and with it the likelihood of winds gusting up to 100mph. When the gales finally hit the country they caused chaos, leaving seven people dead and widespread destruction.

Across the north west the hurricane wreaked havoc in towns and villages. Hundreds of people had to be evacuated from their homes in Wigan and were forced to spend the night in community centres. In Bury, the storm blew the roof off the town hall while the television transmitter on Winter Hill broke down, interrupting a screening of *Conduct Unbecoming* on BBC2. February 9, 1988, would go down in record books as the worst storm to hit Lancashire in a generation, leaving a trail of devastation in its wake.

Marie McCourt had been planning to head into Liverpool city centre to meet her daughter Helen for lunch. She was due to drop off her mother for a hospital appointment and the two would kill time by having a bite to eat and doing a bit of shopping. But after hearing the weather report, Marie cancelled the lunch meeting and headed straight home, wary of delaying her drive in the worsening weather.

Old Hall Street in the heart of Liverpool's business district lies close to the banks of the River Mersey. When the worst of winter's storm clouds roll in from the Irish Sea, the winds have been known to lift those unfortunate enough to venture out on to the street off their feet. Helen McCourt worked as a computer clerk at the Royal Insurance company's head office on the famous old street and when she left work at 4pm the storm was already showing its teeth. Before leaving, she had phoned her mum to let her know what time she would be home and to ask for tea to be ready.

Helen had been seeing a new boyfriend and planned to be home by 5.30pm for a quick wash and change of clothes before heading back out again to meet him for 8pm. A short time later she called again to see if she could borrow her mother's car at the weekend. Marie laughed and said they would discuss it when Helen got home. The pair enjoyed a close relationship and most days Helen would telephone Marie before setting off for the 15-mile journey home from work.

She jumped on the 4.16pm train from Liverpool's Lime Street station to Preston, calling in at St Helens Shaw Street where she arrived in plenty of time to make the 362 Ribble Bus for the final leg of her daily journey home to Billinge. She lived with her mother and younger brother Michael, 19, in the former pit and stone quarrying community on the road between St Helens and Wigan. To fill the time before catching the bus, Helen nipped into the Superdrug shop near to the bus station and bought some toiletries.

After boarding the single-decker bus outside the Theatre Royal at 5pm, she chatted to a number of fellow passengers she recognised during the 15-minute bus ride, before reaching her stop where Rainford Road meets Main Street in Billinge. From there it was 500 yards to her front door.

She alighted in the storm-lashed street and was never seen again.

Helen McCourt was the sort of ordinary, caring daughter that any mum dreams of having. She was born on July 29, 1965, at Balliol Road Hospital in Bootle, and her childhood was spent in Bryn, near

The bus stop in Main Street, Billinge, where Helen McCourt was last seen.

Wigan, where she went to Rose Hill Infants' School, Our Lady's Juniors' and, after the family moved to Billinge in 1979, to St Edmund Arrowsmith High at Ashton. She nurtured a childhood ambition to be a nurse and, needing good qualifications, she continued her studies to pick up six O-levels at St John Rigby College, Orrell. But it was after leaving there that her career took an unexpected turn.

She worked for a spell at Wigan dole office and then went to work at Springfield Hospital, London, not as a nurse, but in the office. It was the first time Helen had lived away and she got terribly homesick and eventually came back to Billinge, moving in with her mum. For more than two years she worked happily at Royal Insurance.

She was a very sociable young woman and the job suited her down to the ground simply because of all the friends she made. The company was renowned in Liverpool for its social scene, with Friday night the highlight of the week for the predominantly young staff who would venture out together in groups to enjoy the city's pubs and clubs.

Even as a youngster Helen had been happy-go-lucky and seemed to manage with a lot less sleep than other children. She always kept herself busy, putting herself forward as a babysitter, and loved dancing as well as doing sponsored walks and fun runs. In the evenings the brunette took up part-time work as an Avon representative advising friends and neighbours on cosmetics to supplement her income.

Although her parents had divorced in 1984, she had a good relationship with both of them and visited her lorry driver father, Billy, in St Helens whenever she wanted. When Helen failed to return home from work on time on that stormy February night a mother's instinct told Marie McCourt something

" ...a mother's instinct told Marie McCourt something was wrong. "

was wrong. Her daughter was punctual and meticulous in her habits and would have telephoned if she had been held up along the way. She always arrived home at 5.50pm. By 7pm alarm bells were ringing.

Marie, 44, was prone to worrying. Had the wild weather caused an accident? Was Helen injured somewhere? Marie had heard on the news that a tree had been blown across the railway line. She telephoned the station and was assured that services were running on schedule between Liverpool and St Helens. The tree was only affecting services further along the route between St Helens and Wigan. She called local hospitals but no-one fitting the 22-year-old's description had been admitted. She telephoned Helen's friends to see if anyone had heard from her or if, perhaps, she'd had a late change of plan and called in to see them.

Nothing.

Helen's boyfriend Frank Palimieri called shortly after 8pm to check their plans were still on for the evening despite the storm. When he learned she had not arrived home, Frank got in the car and drove from his own home, four miles away in Rainford, over to the McCourt house.

Marie kept up her efforts on the telephone. At 9.30pm, her daughter's dinner still on the table, she rang the police and was advised to call again in half an hour. She could wait no longer, and she and Frank drove into Liverpool to retrace Helen's steps.

They cruised past the Royal Insurance offices and called at hospitals to see if she had been admitted. Eventually they pulled up at Copperas Hill police station close to Lime Street railway station where Marie showed officers a photograph of her missing daughter. She also gave a detailed description of the jewellery Helen was wearing and her clothing. She had been wearing opal and sapphire earrings, and matching pendant and ring with the same stones. They were part of a set bought for her 21st birthday. The desk sergeant initially suggested Helen had probably just gone for a few drinks with friends and would probably be in touch. But Marie broke down in tears and explained about the phone calls and that Helen would have told her if she'd had a change of plan.

The police reacted with uncharacteristic haste given they were dealing with a missing person of adult age who had only been gone a few hours. They telexed an immediate appeal for information about Helen throughout the region. It was to prove vital.

The officer told Marie she could telephone him every hour when she arrived home if she wished and promised to alert his colleagues when they arrived for duty. Marie and Frank drove back to Billinge. But she could not sleep and at 4am a police car pulled up outside her red and white detached home. A mother's nightmare had begun.

After getting off the bus, Helen had not called in to the local newsagents around the corner to get a newspaper as she normally would. As people hurried to get home in the wintry weather, no-one noticed what she did next. But one thing is clear: she ended up in her local pub, the George and Dragon.

The pub was just a short walk from where Helen stepped off the bus at the bottom of Main Street and little over half way along her short journey home. She had worked as a barmaid at the pub for a couple of months in 1987 and was a familiar face among the crowd who drank there. The George and Dragon was at the hub of local life for the village's twenty-something crowd and late nights could turn into raucous early morning affairs. After the bell was rung for last orders and the remaining stragglers had set off home, the doors would be bolted and the drinking would continue for the favoured few in the upstairs bar with sessions often going on until dawn.

Landlord Ian Simms would pull the curtains tight to ensure no passing police officer got wind of the revelry underway inside. The stay-behinds were common knowledge among villagers and the police had been called out on several occasions to deal with rowdy behaviour. Most neighbours kept their thoughts to themselves but some complained of drugs being taken in the upstairs bar.

Two days earlier Helen had been enjoying a Sunday night drink at the bar when she became involved in a row with another woman. Janice Smullen had confronted Helen in the pub's toilets after she produced a photograph of Janice's boyfriend with another woman. Simms was called and grabbed Janice by the arm, ordering Helen out of the pub in floods of tears and banning her from returning. She went home and straight to bed. Marie was puzzled at the change in routine as her daughter would usually sit up chatting when she got in from a night out, recalling tales from the evening and passing on bits of gossip she had picked up.

After she left his pub Simms resumed his drinking, telling regulars he hated Helen. What had caused such strength of feeling was not clear although Simms had boasted to at least one friend that he had slept with Helen. His claim was unlikely to be true.

Although she enjoyed a good time, Helen was no good-time girl and up until the previous autumn had been in a long-term relationship. She nurtured dreams of marrying her sweetheart David Haddock until a break up which left her heartbroken.

In the few months since, she had started seeing Frank Palimieri but the couple had never progressed beyond a kiss and a cuddle. But the end of her relationship with David saw Helen spending more time staying out drinking, as she struggled to cope with the split. And after the argument and upset it seems likely that Helen called into the pub on the stormy Tuesday night to speak to Simms to try to smooth things over to ensure she was welcome back.

Within a few minutes of Helen arriving at the George and Dragon, a man getting off a bus outside heard a scream coming from inside the pub which was cut short abruptly as if by a hand being clamped over a mouth. Half an hour later, manageress Maria Glover arrived for work at the adjoining Stone Barn restaurant and heard the sound of someone cleaning coming from next door. Part-time barmaid Karen Tither turned up at the George and Dragon around 7pm and, with no sign of Simms, set to work.

Ian Simms was a keen bodybuilder and Thai boxer.

It was a slow evening with not many people in, and when her boss finally appeared an hour later it was to say he was heading out for half an hour. It was to be closing time when Simms finally reappeared. An uneventful night in the pub was only punctuated by a phone call at 9pm from Marie McCourt. Her daughter Helen had not returned home from work and she was wondering whether she had popped in to the pub on her way home.

Unbeknown to Karen, that is exactly what had happened and where the bubbly insurance clerk had met a violent end.

Ian Simms was a popular figure among the small community of Billinge. After leaving school he worked as a chef at the giant Pilkington Glass works in St Helens for 13 years, where he was also union shop steward. In his spare time he enjoyed fishing with his friends and was a member of a local shooting club for which he owned a number of guns.

At nights he worked as a doorman at the George and Dragon. It was a job which suited his macho image to a tee. A keen bodybuilder and Thai boxer, Simms also saw himself as a bit of a ladies' man and his role on the door gave him plenty of opportunity to try out his chat up lines. Indeed he was not shy of boasting that he could have any woman he chose, such was his confidence in his own sexual magnetism.

It was while working as a bouncer that, in 1986, seeking a change in career, he took over the running of the Stone Barn. When the chance came up to buy the lease of the George and Dragon the following year, he seized the opportunity and quit his post at the restaurant. Once in charge, Simms rarely got his hands dirty working behind the bar, leaving the staff to serve the drinks while he mingled with regulars. Always polite and friendly, the 31-year-old was seen as an unassuming figure from a respectable local family. His only brush with the law came some years earlier with a £10 fine for possession of an air gun in a public place. But beyond the bonhomie, Ian Simms lived a Dr Jekyll and Mr Hyde life.

Behind the back of his trusting wife Nadine, the mother of his two children, he kept a teenage mistress. Simms met Tracey Hornby while working on the door of the pub and before long they were locked in a full-blown affair. The couple would sneak off for secret trysts in hotels in Southport and Windermere. They even managed to spend a week together in Tenerife after Simms concocted an excuse to pretend he had to stay behind at his pub while Nadine went away with the kids.

On the day Helen McCourt vanished, Simms rang Tracey to rearrange their clandestine meeting for the evening. In the previous few months Tracey, who worked as a secretary at an estate agency, increasingly stayed over in the flat above the pub. The 19-year-old had been spending so many nights with Simms that her own mother started to complain that she never spent any time at home.

All the time Nadine was living just around the corner in Birchley Road with their five and six-year-old children and Simms' widowed mother. Her husband would tell her he needed to stay at the pub for security reasons. But each morning he would return home to take the children he doted upon, to and from school. Simms lived in fear of his wife finding out about his affair, while at the same time promising Tracey he would leave Nadine for her.

The pressure to decide between the two women in his life was mounting as news of his liaisons with Tracey slowly became common knowledge among locals. Had Helen angered Simms by passing on gossip about the landlord's secret affair? He certainly thought she had been talking. Pub manager Ronald Carr tipped him off after a local cleaner mentioned it to him. Simms warned Ronald the office girl should be told nothing if she started digging for information.

The next time Helen called into the George and Dragon Simms pulled her to one side to quiz her about the rumours. She denied point blank gossiping about him even when Ronald was called over to repeat what he had heard. Ronald had long been in on the secret. His boss had schooled him that Nadine should never be allowed in the flat and that if she called round when Tracey was ensconced in their love nest, then he was to tell her that Simms was out.

The love-struck teenager would normally call in at the flat at 6pm but on February 9 there was a change of plan. Simms telephoned her and rearranged their rendezvous for 8.30pm.

He had something important he needed to do.

After telling Karen he was nipping out for an hour, Simms reversed his Volkswagen Passat car up to the back gate leading to the outside stairway to his flat. Out of sight he bundled Helen's body into the car boot and set off into the night.

The George and Dragon pub in Billinge where Helen McCourt was murdered by Ian Simms in 1988.

Tracey arrived late as planned and found no sign of Simms in the flat and the door locked. When he finally showed up at 11pm, she was livid and accused him of taking his wife out for dinner. Simms explained he had been to see Nadine and to tell her of their affair. He said she had gone berserk and attacked him leaving scratches on his neck.

Tracey believed him and the two lovers went to bed just yards from where Simms had wrapped a flex around Helen's neck and asphyxiated her just hours earlier.

As they lay in bed Tracey noticed more scratches on his face, chest and legs, scratches which had not been there 24 hours earlier when they last made love. Scratches he claimed Nadine had left in a rage after he had confessed his infidelity. The marks betrayed the desperate battle for life Helen had put up, as she fought with the muscle-bound bodybuilder on the landing carpet.

The hurricane force winds had subsided to a fresh breeze and there was just a gentle rain in the air as the people of Billinge woke up on February 10. Two delivery men doing the morning newspaper run noticed the lights were still on at the George and Dragon as dawn prepared to break over Lancashire.

At that time of the day any sign of life registered during the mundanity of their daily routine. In a village of just 5,410 residents, not much goes unnoticed and word spread quickly of the police car which had been parked outside Marie

McCourt's house since the small hours. Within the space of a few hours Billinge was to find itself at the centre of one of the region's biggest manhunts in years.

Suddenly detectives were swarming all over the village. The old school hall, used only for flower shows and church meetings, was transformed into an operations centre by Merseyside Police. A fleet of more than 30 police vehicles, including horse wagons and dog vans, jostled for space amid the fish vans and bread trucks delivering to the village shops.

Three days a week Mary Smith would turn up at the George and Dragon at 9am to clean the pub. The routine was always the same; she would knock at the door and have to wait around on the street for several minutes for it to be answered. Simms was not an early riser. But that morning the door opened almost straight away, and she was greeted by a grubby looking Simms.

Her first task was always to head for the cleaning cupboard to get her utensils and she found a new supply of plastic bin bags. Strange, she thought, as new supplies had not been ordered. As she set to work cleaning the toilet, Mary could hear someone scrubbing away vigorously at the bottom of the stairs. It was Simms. He told her the dog had fouled the carpet and he was clearing up the mess with bleach.

Across Billinge a 120-strong police team was drafted in to search for Helen McCourt. From the beginning police feared she had been killed. Uniformed officers set off carrying out house-to-house inquiries along the route the pretty young woman would have made towards her own home. Waste skips were scoured, gardens checked, motorists stopped and their vehicles searched while an RAF helicopter, equipped with photographic reconnaissance equipment used in the hunt for the victims of the Moors murders, was called in to help comb the area. At nearby Carr Mill Dam beauty spot, frogmen scoured the waters while dog handlers and mounted police inched through the woodlands searching for any clue as to what had happened to Helen.

Fifteen miles away, butcher Gordon Bannister was out walking his dog on a towpath alongside the Manchester Ship Canal close to his home in the Hollins Green suburb of Warrington when he stumbled across a blood stained towel. Further up on an embankment rising to the A57 he spotted a second towel and several items of discarded men's clothing. A pair of Marks and Spencer underpants, a blue sock, jumper, ankle boots and a crumpled pair of muddy jeans which looked like someone had stepped out of them and left them where they were. He called police who sealed off the spot close to a privately owned tip.

The telex dispatched from Copperas Hill police station the previous evening added extra urgency to their response. The jumper was emblazoned with the promotional logo of Labatts beer, a popular drink at the George and Dragon. The investigation had its first pointer to Ian Simms and its first grim piece of evidence that a missing person probe had become a murder case.

Two of Helen's uncles already had suspicions about the pub landlord after he lied when they quizzed him the evening after their niece vanished. They informed police and on the Thursday police door-to-door inquiries arrived at the George and Dragon. Efforts in the first 24 hours after Helen's disappearance had focused on her close friends, family and single men in the village. The pub was a natural next place to centre police attention as the hub of local life.

Simms was not around when they arrived in the morning.

The search uncovered many clues to the murder, but Helen's body was never found.

When the landlord showed up at 11.30am he told officers he had been to the Irlam and Cadishead Royal British Legion to try to book the club for a private party. He had chosen the venue because he wanted to put exotic dancers on and feared the locals would be unhappy if he tried to stage a strip show at his own pub. Officers fired a few more routine questions at him and one of the policemen noticed the landlord's stomach was palpitating as if with fear and he struggled to get his words out.

Simms was taken to St Helens Police Station to make a statement and while he was being questioned, a forensics officer made the first big breakthrough.
Traces of blood and part of an opal and sapphire earring were found in the boot of Simms' Volkswagen Passat. Police showed the earring to Marie McCourt who confirmed it was part of the set bought for Helen's 21st birthday. Detective

Inspector George Durno broke the news to Simms and arrested him on suspicion of murder.

After 36 hours in custody, detectives were granted permission by a magistrate to hold the man, who was now their prime suspect, for a further 36 hours. He disputed any suggestion as to how the earring had found its way into the boot, claiming he had not seen Helen since the Sunday evening of the row when he had thrown her out. He said the scratch marks on his neck must have been made during the argument in the toilets as he pulled apart Helen and Janice Smullen. Or perhaps they came from brambles as he went out walking his dog each day at Carr Mill Dam. There was no mention of the row with Nadine he had told Tracey was the cause. Later he would claim he was too embarrassed to mention the affair for fear Nadine would really discover his betrayal.

The blood stain in the boot, he added, was made by his dog which had cut its paw while out walking. Someone must have planted his clothes by the canal in Hollins Green to frame him, he argued. When it was pointed out someone had seen his dark blue Volkswagen at the canal at 7.30am on Wednesday, he explained that someone else must have driven his car to the isolated

Scores of residents volunteered to help in the search for Helen McCourt.

spot. The pattern of denials, which was to write the murder into the annals of the nation's most notorious crimes, was under way.

Forensics teams set to work taking apart the landlord's flat. Two fingerprints left in blood were found on the flat door and experts were quickly able to establish at least one belonged to Simms. Traces of blood were also found on the stairs leading up to the flat, a door hinge and in the back bedroom. Simms' discarded clothes also bore traces of blood.

Using the very latest in DNA technology police were able to rule out Simms, Tracey or Nadine as being the source of the blood.

Genetic testing was carried out on samples from Billy, Marie and Michael McCourt and showed the bloodstains were 126,000 times more likely to have come from a member of their family than from anyone else. The same tests on blood samples taken from Simms' clothes found by the canal threw up the same result. Mud found on two of Simms' rings, one of which could only just be removed from his finger, and a bracelet matched in colour mud found on the Passat and the dumped clothes. It suggested he had been up to his wrists, at least, in mud. The case against him was building and on February 14, 1988, Detective Superintendent Paul Ackers formally charged Simms with the murder of Helen McCourt. His response was a simple, "I didn't do it." But police were still baffled as to where the killer had disposed of his victim's body.

While work was underway bringing a case against Simms, scores of officers were involved in the hunt for Helen's remains. On Friday February 12, the man leading the murder investigation, Detective Chief Superintendent Eddie Aldred, made an appeal for help: "We do not know where Helen's body is – it could be anywhere in the north of England.

"We desperately need to know where she is."

Helen McCourt.

The clues lining up against Simms led police to believe Helen's body lay in a shallow grave of clay surrounded by brambles and gorse. Det Chief Supt Aldred asked for volunteers willing to join a search of the vast expanse of fields, waterways and woodland around Billinge to assemble outside St Aidan's Church Hall, in Main Street, at 10.30am the following day equipped with waterproof clothes and rubber boots. The response amazed police.

Around 2,000 people defied wet weather to turn up, including local Scout groups and soldiers from the 238 squadron of the Royal Corps of Transport, based in Bootle, who decided to combine a planned map reading exercise with the hunt. Many people were turned away as police struggled to corral the huge turn out. Those 600 members of the public who remained were divided up into groups of between 10 and 20 to fan out across a wide area of farmland and nearby fields, each led by police officers.

Ditches, woodland and flooded pits were all scoured for any sign of disturbance in an operation which lasted all weekend. Detective Superintendent Tom Davies told the *Lancashire Evening Post*, "There is no doubt that all those volunteers did us a tremendous service in helping to eliminate vast tracts of land around Billinge which would have taken us a lot longer to do unassisted by the public."

On the Sunday morning, schoolchildren and worshippers offered special prayers for Helen at church services in Billinge and Orrell.

With Simms in custody and maintaining his denial the mass search threw up no hint of where he had hidden Helen's body. Geologists were drafted in to match soil and clay samples taken from hedges, ditches and quarries across the area with those recovered from his car, the jewellery and clothes. With local farmland dotted with long forgotten pit shafts and flooded mine workings and a lot of the higher ground overgrown, they faced a mammoth challenge despite assistance from old Coal Board maps. Around Billinge the search spread over thousands of acres.

Ian Simms.

One week on from Helen's disappearance, police staged a reconstruction in the village of the insurance worker's last known movements in the hope of jogging someone's memory. A local part-time model with an uncanny resemblance to Helen caught the same 362 bus from St Helens to Billinge wearing similar clothes – a long beige overcoat, maroon scarf and brown leather boots – and carrying a red carrier bag. Getting off the bus she traced the steps Helen would normally have taken on her way home into Main Street.

The model, Lisa Shell, agreed to take part in the reconstruction after detectives spotted her in the street and noted how much she looked like the missing villager. The 18-year-old was among the volunteers who had turned up en masse to help the search the previous weekend and was turned away because there were too many people willing to help.

Almost one month later fitness instructor David Farrell was out shooting rats with an air rifle when he discovered a woman's blue handbag behind Irlam swimming baths close to the edge of the old course of the River Irwell. Among the personal effects inside the bag were credit cards, make up and a receipt from Superdrug. Thinking it may have been thrown from a passing car, David took it to a local police station but there was no-one there. He took the bag home and with his parents they searched through it for any clue as to its owner.

When they found a card with a photograph of Helen McCourt and her name on it they realised the significance of the discovery and telephoned the police.

The following morning the scene was cordoned off and over the following two days officers found Helen's purse, a pair of ladies' knickers, a pair of ladies' blue jeans and Helen's missing earring, beige coat, maroon scarf and green mittens in a black bin bag.

They also recovered a grey jacket, a packet of opened crisps, Helen's diary, an accounts book, novel, letters, a bus ticket and a piece of electrical flex. As well as Helen's clothes the bin bag contained all of the items detailed on the Superdrug receipt bar one.

Police had found everything the missing office worker had with her and everything she was wearing the last time she was seen, apart from the toothbrush she had bought an hour before her disappearance. The flex had been twisted into a knot and had human hairs entangled in it.

The spot was less than three miles from where Simms' clothing had been found four weeks earlier on the banks of the Manchester Ship Canal and just one mile from Irlam and Cadishead Royal British Legion where he told police he had been the morning of his arrest. Police divers were called in to search the stretch of the Irwell for any sign of Helen's body. The find was to help paint the most likely portrait of what happened to Helen McCourt on the evening of February 9, 1988. Scientists compared the hair samples to strands removed from her set of rollers and produced a perfect match. Fibres found on her coat were identical to those on the landing carpet at the George and Dragon.

Forensic scientist Dr Eric Moore concluded that the large number of fibres indicated a "prolonged and forceful" contact between the coat and the carpet. Helen had clearly been dragged across the floor of Simms' flat. Fibres from her coat were also found in the car boot, while fibres from her mittens were picked out on Simms' grey coat. Her blood stains found earlier revealed she had been assaulted close to the flat's rear door. The same area the passerby remembered hearing a blood curdling scream just minutes after Helen was last seen getting off the 362 bus from St Helens.

The nature of blood spots and splashes on the door showed Helen had been punched nearby. Dead or alive, she was then dragged into the back bedroom by her arms, ripping the lining of her coat at the seams. The hairs removed from the flex indicated it had been wrapped around Helen's neck and used to strangle her. Some strands were broken, others had been ripped out at the root showing the force used to yank the ligature tight.

Simms admitted owning the flex and even pointed to teeth marks along its length made by his dog to show how he could be sure it was his. He also acknowledged the grey coat belonged to him as well.

Forensic teams returned to his flat and found the missing Superdrug toothbrush which had not previously seemed relevant to their investigation. They also made two further discoveries on the back bedroom carpet which were to prove much more damning – a clump of Helen's hair and the butterfly clip from the earring officers had earlier found in the boot of Simms' car.

In the weeks which followed a Spear and Jackson spade was found in Rixton, near Warringon. It belonged to Ian Simms. The area was close to the private tip where Helen's clothes were discovered. A bulldozer was brought in to skim the top surface off a farmer's field in case the body was lying in a shallow grave. Tracker dogs were employed to search drainage ditches around the farm and a nearby water-filled clay pit was examined.

Still denying any knowledge of Helen's disappearance, one year and 13 days after she went missing Ian Simms went on trial at Liverpool Crown Court accused of her murder.

Over the following three weeks the court heard ground-breaking details of how the very latest DNA science had been able to transform the clothes found dumped on two waterside paths into a dossier of damning evidence against the father-of-two.

Experts from Home Office laboratories at Chorley and Aldermaston, Berkshire, performed sophisticated grouping and make-up tests, some only just pioneered, on the traces of blood. By carefully comparing every microscopic detail with samples of the blood from Helen's parents and brother they were able to draw the same conclusions.

It was Helen's blood.

Many of the tests were carried out independently, sometimes requiring only a spot of blood the size of a pinhead. They examined tiny material fibres found in the flat, the car and on the clothes. Other experts examined mud found on the clothes, in the car and on the spade found at Rixton. They tested 600 soil samples in an effort to discover its origin.

Jurors, lawyers, trial judge Mr Justice Caulfield and a handcuffed Simms were taken to visit the two sites and given a tour of the George and Dragon as prosecutors sought to lift the lid on where, and crucially, at whose hands Helen had met her fate. Although closed and boarded up after the murder, the pub's landing carpet was re-laid to give jurors an insight as to how it looked the night of the killing.

Police surgeon Dr Miles Clark revealed he had examined Simms three days after Helen went missing and found numerous fine scratches on his body, legs and arms. Some, he believed, were left by fingernails others by brambles. But still the landlord denied killing Helen.

The clothes found at Hollins Green were not his, he claimed, and must have been placed there by someone keen to frame him. When reminded his car was seen at the same spot, he said that same person must have borrowed his keys, as his friends often did, and driven it there. Simms claimed he spent the wild and stormy night when Helen vanished sitting on Southport beach in tears as he contemplated the mental torment of his tangled love life.

After denying in police interviews his victim had ever been in his flat, the serial womaniser alleged she had once nipped upstairs for "a kiss and a cuddle", and that would explain the wealth of forensic evidence placing her there.

When Tracey Hornby took her turn on the stand she revealed she and Simms had discussed Helen's disappearance in the hours before her lover's arrest and what may have happened to her. "He was as shocked as I was," she told jurors.

And she spoke of her continuing love for the man in the dock despite the gravity of the charge he faced. "He always told me that he was not just messing me about, but that he did not want to upset his mother who lived with Nadine. I know that he did intend to leave her."

Tracey may have believed Simms' lies but the five men and seven women of the jury saw straight through his web of deceit.

On March 14, 1989, following a 16-day trial, they took just five-and-a-half hours to return a unanimous guilty verdict to cheers and applause from the McCourt family. Marie had attended every day of the hearing, often reduced to tears as she sat in a special area reserved for relatives. On that final day she was wearing a black and blue check suit which belonged to Helen. It made her feel closer to Helen, she said. A devout Catholic, she clutched prayer cards and a drawing of the Madonna and Child as she listened to the harrowing evidence.

Mr Justice Caulfield summed up the case by describing Simms as being "in the first division of cold blooded murderers." After the verdict was returned he summoned the killer to his feet and told him, "This jury, after long and grave deliberations, has decided that you took the life of this young, happy girl and having taken her life that you have hidden or desecrated her body so that her parents can never respect her corpse."

❝ ...you took the life of this young, happy girl. ❞

Jurors and court officials visit the spot where Helen's clothes were discovered.

"You have cast her garments virtually to the rats and you have stripped yourself in another obscure place. You have done that coldly and callously and you have shown no remorse."

As Simms was sentenced to life, pandemonium broke out in the court room as members of Helen's family tried to attack the man who killed their loved one. Her brother Michael leaped from his seat and had to be restrained by his dad Billy as he shouted, "I'll wait for you Simms. I'll get you."

Unrepentant as ever Simms was led to the cells proclaiming his innocence, "I never touched her, I never seen her."

Speaking after the trial Det Chief Supt Eddie Aldred explained how the speed with which Helen's disappearance had been identified as something far more sinister than a missing person inquiry was the key to solving an investigation that cost £250,000. He told the *Evening Post*, "The fact that Helen's disappearance was reported so early was very important to us."

"People go missing all the time, but because of the type of person we knew her to be, and the fact she had already rung home on that night to say what time she would be in, we treated it as a major incident. If another 24 hours had elapsed, Simms could have washed the mud, which proved so important, off his car and may also have found and got rid of the earring in the boot, which was another vital clue for us."

The case made legal history as only the third time a contested trial had been brought and a conviction secured without a victim's body, and the first through the use of DNA fingerprinting. But despite Simms' conviction, more than two decades later the misery continues for the McCourt family.

Helen's body has never been recovered and for years after she vanished relatives spent every spare hour of their weekends trudging through the countryside searching for any sign of her remains. In the weeks after she went missing four of Helen's uncles took one month off work to continue the hunt. By June they were unable to prevent Marie from joining them any longer.

The trial provided new leads and new hope as they learned of more possible sites where Simms might have dumped Helen's corpse that storm lashed night. Aided by a computer donated by Helen's bosses the family mounted a systematic search of remote areas the killer could conceivably have reached in the time he had available to cover his tracks.

Initially they concentrated upon areas close to the Manchester Ship Canal at which blood stained clothing and the spade were found but they ventured further afield to Stoke-on-Trent and Ellesmere Port. Help came from many quarters, people with metal detectors, water divining experts and mediums all offered their support.

As if the family's suffering was not great enough Simms lodged an appeal over the conduct of his trial claiming Mr Justice Caulfield had misled the jury. His appeal was thrown out. And still he refused to say where Helen's body was hidden.

In 1991, in desperation, Marie McCourt wrote and hand delivered to the gates of Wakefield Prison a letter to her daughter's killer pleading with him to give up his dark secret. In it she said,

> It is now just over three years since I last saw my darling daughter's beautiful, smiling face. Three years since I heard her lovely voice and infectious laughter, but it only seems like yesterday, vivid in my mind and in my memory.

The letter went on to outline the fruitless weekly searches by Helen's loved ones for her remains:

They have crawled through rat infested tunnels and drains, gone down old mine workings, waded chest deep in canals and ponds. They have strimmed and fingertip searched acres of wasteland, moved mountains of rubbish and checked hundreds of black plastic bin bags. They have cleared a mineshaft of rubble with their bare hands to a depth of 24 feet and have dug with spades for mile after mile and still, for my sake and Helen's, we will go on looking for as long as it takes.

You are now serving a life sentence for Helen's murder and until you show remorse and admit what you have done, that life sentence will mean precisely what it says – LIFE.

The letter failed to stir Simms' conscience.

Marie McCourt then turned to the law in an effort to force Simms to reveal his secret and allow Helen the full Christian burial service she was desperate to have. She invoked a legal statute dating back to 1788, which created the crime of Preventing a Christian Burial. It was not as archaic as it sounds. In 1996, one of the ten life sentences handed down to Scottish child killer Robert Black was for this offence after he concealed the bodies of his victims Sarah Harper, Susan Maxwell and Caroline Hogg.

In 1999 Marie held a meeting with Home Secretary Jack Straw and presented him with a video detailing the story of her daughter's murder, which included stills of the locations where the family had searched for Helen's body, and told him of her heartbreak at not being able to give her daughter a Christian burial. They discussed the 18th century legislation and also powers to prosecute Simms for preventing a coroner from carrying out his lawful duty. But Mr Straw was unable to help.

Ian Simms failed in a bid for parole in February 2007 and remains behind bars. He still has never admitted where Helen's remains are hidden.

Marie now works as a co-ordinator for Support after Murder and Manslaughter, visiting families who have experienced the same ordeal of losing a loved one to murder. Her second husband John Sandwell is chairman of the group. The couple still spend weekends looking for Helen's body.

CHAPTER SEVEN

Killer in the doll's house

Margaret Lowther, Morecambe, February 17, 1988

CAROL Lowther had chores to complete. There was washing to do and packing to take care of. In two days' time the family were planning to up sticks and move from their home on Morecambe's Mellishaw Caravan Park to a new site in Stockton-on-Tees. As travellers, they had decided to leave the seaside town behind for the north east. Carol's husband James was in talks with the site warden over a new caravan for the move.

The couple had only been at the park since November but had itchy feet. Despite enjoying their stay in Lancashire they were looking forward to a move, which would bring them nearer to James' family. Their last stop off had been in Middlesbrough and it was a part of the country they knew well.

The couple first met there as teenagers when Carol moved to be with her brothers and sisters. When the time came to move on, James followed her all of the way to her sister's caravan in Wakefield and surprised her with a knock on the door. He asked her out and they had been together ever since.

The highlight of their brief time at Mellishaw came at Christmas when they bought a big tree and dressed it with coloured lights. Their eldest child Margaret had happily called her Nannie from the red telephone box at the end of the lane to tell her all of the things she wanted from Santa Claus. And duly on the big day, a parcel arrived full of clothes and a new quilt.

In common with most of the caravans parked off Mellishaw Lane, there was no room for the washing facilities taken for granted in most homes, so Carol was busy using the big twin tub housed in the park's wash shed in preparation for the move. With three small children and a husband to look after there was plenty of washing to do and the young mum was laden with three black bin bags full of clothes.

Back in the caravan Margaret was pushing her four-month-old brother James backwards and forwards in his pram to try to get him off to sleep. The five-year-old was a girly-girl, and loved playing with prams and dolls and doted on her baby brother. She dressed her black, curly-haired doll with his clothes and would happily play for hours with her favourite toy.

Council welfare officers would call in to see the family as part of their weekly round to check everything was alright with the children living at Mellishaw. They would remark on how happy and well adjusted Margaret was, and how extremely well Carol and James cared for their little girl. When Carol got back to her caravan on Plot G she started folding up Margaret's clothes and putting them in a cupboard to dry. When they first arrived in Morecambe the family had shared a small caravan but more recently had moved into a larger static home. Royal Doulton dolls lined the shelves and there was a small kitchen area for cooking. Carol was proud of the caravan and kept it as homely as she could with vases of fresh flowers on the table.

The travelling community at Mellishaw was a tight-knit group with many of the residents related. Carol had been brought up in a travelling family and had seven brothers and six sisters. It was the only world she knew and the 24-year-old felt comfortable knowing she was surrounded by the people closest to her. Margaret's cousins lived in the caravan next door and as Carol busied herself tidying around, her daughter asked if she could pop around to see them and watch a video. They had tapes of *Worzel Gummidge* and she loved to laugh along with the television favourite's antics.

It was mid-February and the weather was bitterly cold and windy outside. Recent weeks had seen stormy weather lash the Lancashire coast and the site was in a muddy state. Carol was not keen on the idea of the girl, affectionately known as Maga, venturing out alone. But her husband had arrived home and persuaded Carol to let little Maga go as it was only next door, and while she was out it would give them extra space to prepare for the move.

Travellers first began to park up on land off Mellishaw Lane in 1974 developing a temporary campsite. The area lies in a remote spot at Heaton with Oxcliffe midway between Lancaster and Morecambe and close to the western bank of the River Lune.

Frequent flooding led to the plot being closed down after just 18 months and many of the community then set up illegal pitches on Morecambe's White Lund industrial estate where they could pick up casual work and peddle scrap metal.

North Lancashire has long been a favourite stopping-off point for travellers particularly during the summer months when hundreds of gypsies and travellers head for Appleby for the traditional horse fair. With more than 100 families sometimes parked up on the White Lund, Lancashire County Council decided to build a permanent campsite.

Mellishaw Caravan Park was opened in 1983 with 19 pitches and separate amenities blocks housing shower rooms, toilets, cooking facilities and hot and cold water. With hook-up facilities for each plot providing electricity, it was part of the modern network of secure, purpose-built travellers' sites provided by the county council. Families seeking to set up home there had to apply to Lancaster City Council, sign a lease agreement and pay weekly site fees.

Close to a rubbish tip on one side, and less than half a mile from the shores of the Lune on the other, it is hidden away down a tiny lane. Most of the caravans were statics but the odd trailer home and traditional wooden caravan were parked in an arc around a large circular mound of grass at the heart of the site. A dilapidated but traditional red-painted wooden gypsy caravan welcomed visitors at the entrance to the site.

It was a popular site, particularly with members of the Irish travelling community, and by 1988 the park had become mainly residential, with most of the families setting up home on a long-term basis. Council officials had worked closely with the National Gypsy Council to create the park and it was considered a successful venture with nearby residents accepting the travellers into the community. Many of the men were regulars in the local pubs, while the women would use nearby shops. All mixed easily with locals. Children living on the park were happily enrolled at schools across the area. Such was the success of Mellishaw, there was a long waiting list for places and turnover of families was slow.

Maga knocked on the door of the neighbouring caravan and asked if her cousin Coralina Johnston wanted to come out and play in the doll's house. The doll's house was really a makeshift shed behind the caravans and close to the perimeter of the campsite.

It was a popular place for the children to go and play and the girls' parents would have been happy the pair would be safe in there. All of the youngsters who lived in Mellishaw Park were taught by their parents never to leave the site and never to go off without a parent or someone they knew well. Providing a caring and safe environment for children is enshrined in the culture of travellers, with adults particularly protective of young girls.

As the two cousins played in the doll's house they were joined by another of their cousins, John Johnston. The two girls set about playing house and making a

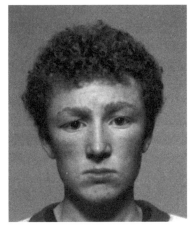

pretend dinner as the elder Johnston sat silently in the corner and watched. Before long it was teatime for real, and Coralina's mother called out across the park for her to come home. The nine-year-old said goodbye and skipped off home, leaving Maga alone with her 17-year-old cousin.

Johnston asked Maga if she wanted to go the shop with him to buy some sweets and fizzy pop. Although her mum was making tea for her back in the caravan, the youngster agreed and the cousins set off into the darkness. Squeezing through a gap in the

Child killer John Johnston.

perimeter fence they headed off across the rain sodden fields in the direction of the nearby Asda store which was less than a mile away and the nearest shop to Mellishaw.

Maga never made it.

Around 250 yards from the safety of the camp, in the wintry darkness Johnston pounced on his young cousin. Ripping off her little red ski pants, white knickers, ankle socks and trainers he launched a horrific sexual assault on the five-year-old. As he carried out the vile attack, he pushed Maga's face into a pool of mud to stifle her cries.

The youngster fought desperately for her life but had no chance against the might of a teenager on the brink of manhood.

Johnston had already decided she must be silenced to ensure she could not tell her mum and dad what he had done. Maga gulped in mouthfuls of mud as she battled vainly to breathe but against the strength of her older cousin she could not survive. She died at 6pm on Wednesday, February 17.

John Johnston lived on the next plot to Carol and James Lowther and their three children with his uncle Ronnie Price. They were already encamped at Mellishaw when the Lowthers arrived three months previously to be nearer to Carol's family. On the other side of Johnston's van, his mother Davina lived with Johnston's stepfather, William Johnston, and their two young children. Such was the intertwined family relationships on the park, William was Carol's brother. It was Davina and William's caravan where Maga had told her mum she was going to watch videos when she popped out before tea.

Known to his family as Riggie, at 5ft 6in tall, John Johnston cut a slight figure who stood out because of his mop of red curly hair and his habit of always dressing in a collared shirt. He was born in Muirhead, Scotland, and was known as a bit of a loner around the site.

Growing up he rarely played with the other children, preferring to keep the company of his sisters. Most travellers viewed him as a bit simple and slow, and as a child his parents rarely let him out of their sight. He never held down a full-time job and instead passed his days collecting scrap metal, returning at night to the caravan they shared.

Johnston had spent the early part of the day out and about collecting unwanted pieces of metal from local businesses with his uncle. They returned to Mellishaw in the afternoon to sort through the bits of scrap they had picked up. Happy with their haul, they went to a local dealer to cash in on the scrap metal. It was a routine familiar to the two men and once they collected their money the whole family headed into Morecambe to do the weekly shop before returning to their caravan for tea.

Johnston didn't eat much and announced he was not really hungry. He left the table and walked out of the caravan and headed for the doll's house where he met Maga and Coralina. After killing his little cousin, Johnston readjusted his clothes and continued his journey across the fields to Asda.

❝ After killing his little cousin, Johnston readjusted his clothes and continued his journey... ❞

Once at the supermarket he headed for the confectionary aisle, picked up a couple of chocolate bars, a bottle of pop and headed to the till. Check-out worker Diane Nash noticed Johnston looked scruffy as she totted up his bill, but he was calm and

Frank Keating, the Post's new star columnist - Back Page

MONSTER

Gas blast victims' court victory

By TONY SKINNER

THE victims of the Abbeystead disaster have won their second legal battle for justice. The Court of Appeal in

£½m SKI DREAM - PAGE 9

The Mellishaw caravan site where Margaret lived. Parents had warned children not to leave without permission

Pylon

there was nothing to betray the horror of what he had just done. She packed his shopping into a carrier bag and handed him his till receipt, which was stamped 6.25pm.

As the 5.45pm news came on the television, Carol Lowther left the chicken soup she was cooking on the hob and went to the door of her caravan to call Maga in for her tea. When there was no reply her husband James told her not to worry and to leave her out playing and walked across to speak to the camp warden about the new caravan he was looking for.

But Carol could not settle and stayed at the door shouting over and again for Maga to come home. When there was no sign of her little daughter she went out to see if perhaps she had fallen asleep in the back of the family car. She then spotted her niece Coralina and and asked her where her Maga was. Coralina, who was known as Lena by her family, said she had seen her heading off in the direction of the shops with John Johnston. An involuntary chill ran down Carol's spine.

Maga would never leave the site with someone else without telling her mum. Carol began screaming for Maga to come home. The panic in her voice roused residents across Mellishaw to come out to see what the commotion was. Friends and family started scouring the site looking in their own cars and caravans to see if the little girl could have slipped inside unnoticed.

Johnston's stepfather William and uncle Ronnie Price were looking around the camp gate when they came across Johnston on his way back from Asda and asked him if he had seen Maga. He replied, "No". The three of them started walking towards Johnston's caravan and, thinking she could see Maga there, Carol ran over, relieved her daughter was safe but angry that she had disappeared without letting her know.

But the little girl was not with the men. Still clutching his Asda bag Carol looked Johnston in the eye and asked him where Maga was. Without hesitating, he said he had left her at the shop. For some reason she could not comprehend, Carol could not keep her eyes off his carrier bag as if it contained some clue as to where the youngster was.

Carol and her brother headed off through the camp's only proper entrance and along the unlit lane towards the shop, still calling out for Maga.

By now she was hysterical and everything around her was a blur. Somebody wrapped a blanket around her shoulders as voices urged her to keep calm, not to worry, that everything would be alright. There was no sign of Maga in the lane or at Asda. When they returned to the park there was a crowd of people around the warden's caravan at the bottom of the site. As they stumbled towards the caravan, Carol saw the paramedics rushing inside. But no-one would let her follow.

As Carol had set off up Mellishaw Lane to look for her daughter, Johnston had joined another uncle, Ongie Price, to search for his missing cousin in his car. The two drove slowly down the lane and Johnston suggested they pull in to a lay-by off nearby Ovangle Road. There was a fire burning on a waste tip close by and Johnston climbed up over the tip alone to carry out a search.

He had only been out of sight a few minutes when he cried out to Ongie, and as his uncle raced over, Johnston appeared from the darkness with a body wrapped in his grey coat in his arms. He explained that he had seen a man about 20 yards away carrying Maga across the tip. Johnston said he had sworn at the man who, startled, had dropped the little girl and run off.

In that moment, he decided not to chase the man but instead dropped to his knees to try to talk to Maga. There was no answer. The men placed Maga in the passenger seat of Ongie's car and shook her in an attempt to rouse her. Arriving back at the park in the car, they carried her to Johnston's mother Davina, who carried her niece to the warden's caravan. Johnston turned to Ongie and said, "They've killed her" and the pair headed back to find the men he claimed he had seen by the fire down the road.

Someone dialled 999 while others tried to resuscitate the child. Paramedics arrived and battled to bring Maga back to life but it was too late. The trusting little girl had died in the darkness, face down in a muddy field, just yards from her family and safety.

Eventually Carol managed to force her way into the caravan. She was met by a scene of unimaginable horror. Her precious daughter lay half naked on the floor, her blonde ringlets sodden with mud and her legs tilted to an angle. She was surrounded by resuscitation machines pumping up and down with paramedics at her side.

Unable to comprehend what she was seeing, Carol thought her daughter was breathing. But it was the vain attempts of the medics seeking to get her little lungs working again on their own.

She kept asking what was going on, why was Maga undressed? Maga was a modest child and would not even let her father see her without her clothes on at bath time. She was always wary of strangers and would certainly never have wandered off with someone she did not know.

Carol took the blanket from her shoulders and tenderly placed it across her daughter's waist. As the paramedics kept up their efforts for a further few minutes, James burst in. He had been off the site and unaware of the tragic events unfolding as he made his way back.

A policeman and policewoman calmly asked the Lowthers to step outside the caravan. They closed the door behind them and quietly broke the dreadful news, "There's something we need to tell you – your daughter's dead."

❝ There's something we need to tell you – your daughter's dead. ❞

In shock, Carol and James were driven away to Morecambe police station. Throughout the short journey Carol kept asking where they were going, pleading with the officers to take them back, that Maga needed them, that she would be wondering where they were. But despite her distressed state, Carol was able to point the finger at Johnston.

More than 50 detectives were drafted in to the join hunt for Maga's killer and an incident room was opened at Morecambe police station. The operation was headed by Detective Superintendent Bill Hacking, one of Lancashire's most experienced murder squad detectives. At dawn officers fanned out across the camp site and surrounding fields, cordoning off strips of land with wooden staves and orange tape to look for any clue as to what had happened to Maga in the missing hour which claimed her young life. Her clothes were still missing and police were sure their discovery would point a finger towards her killer. Vehicles travelling into the campsite and area were stopped, the occupants quizzed and car registrations logged.

Car loads of grim-faced travellers came and went all day, while inside the camp a group of children innocently played ring-a-roses nearby, oblivious to the terrifying fate which had claimed their playmate. Fear gripped the nation as news of Maga's death hit the television bulletins.

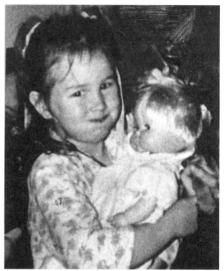

Margaret Lowther, photographed two months before she died.

Throughout the 1980s a child killer had stalked northern England and Scotland, claiming the lives of three little girls. Susan Maxwell, Caroline Hogg and Sarah Harper had all been snatched, raped and murdered, their bodies dumped on wasteland. Immediately people feared the serial killer had struck again. Parents in Morecambe and Lancaster were advised to pick their children up from school and those youngsters unable to be collected were ordered to walk home in groups.

But police in Lancashire already had their prime suspect and they needed to act quickly. Detectives feared he could travel on and never be found again. Or worse still, angry travellers would arrive at the same conclusion and seek to mete out their own justice.

Johnston was arrested and taken to Morecambe police station for questioning.

As he was still a juvenile in the eyes of the law, his parents and a representative from social services were required to be present throughout the interview process. Davina Johnston visited her son several times in the cells to speak with him alone. He told her he could not stomach the allegations being put to him by detectives and was frightened he was going to admit to murder.

But after her third visit to the cells he began to confess what he had done, telling his mother if she believed he had carried out the horrific crime then he would admit it. At first Johnston claimed he had not seen Maga at all, then changed his story to say he did not kill his little cousin but had stumbled across her body and had sex with her corpse. Officers knew the confession was a lie and pressed ahead with their interrogation.

Finally, Johnston confessed.

> **He admitted killing his little cousin.**

He admitted killing his little cousin but told investigators it was an accident. The teenager said Maga had deliberately "turned him on" and had taken off her own clothes. He described how they had been having sex and the child's face was in the mud. When he pulled her up, Johnston claimed, he realised she was dead.

It was one final sickening lie piling insult on to the unimaginable heartache he had brought to his extended family. Throughout the confession, the killer's appalled parents were sat alongside him listening to every harrowing detail.

The following day Johnston was taken back to Mellishaw by detectives to search for Maga's missing clothes and pinpoint the murder scene. But he was spotted by a group of angry travellers and police were forced to retreat and bundle him back in the car and speed off. His family's caravan was vandalised and they fled the site and headed back to Ireland. Unable to hold his head up in public, Carol's father died of a broken heart, grief stricken and unable to comprehend the horrific truth that his grandson had killed his beautiful granddaughter.

The Lowthers turned their back on Mellishaw as well, leaving immediately for their new home at Preston Lane Camp in Stockton. Neither family ever returned to Mellishaw. In line with travellers' tradition, the Lowthers' caravan was burned to the ground along with the doll's house and a cart the children used to play on. Carol's sister also burned all of her niece's clothes.

At 4pm on the day after the murder, police found Maga's clothes on marshland 40 yards from where the youngster had been killed. It was to prove crucial for

The search for evidence.

detectives in nailing Johnston. Two days after the terrible killing Johnston was brought before Lancaster Magistrates Court to face the charge of murder. He was sped to court from Morecambe police station flanked by motorcycle outriders to stop the traffic as a convoy of several vehicles, all with lights flashing and klaxons wailing, tore through the heart of Lancaster en routeto the court.

The resort's own magistrates court, situated down a narrow side street, had closed some years previously and all judicial matters for the town had been transferred to the then-newly constructed court building in Lancaster situated across from the main police station. When the door leading from the cells opened and the accused entered the room, the only sign of the killer visible to the waiting media pack was a mop of red hair. John Johnston was so small that he could only just see over the lip of the dock.

The hearing lasted less than five minutes and there was no application for bail before he was whisked off to HMP Risley on remand. Maga's funeral took place six weeks later on March 3, 1988, in Stockton with 1,000 mourners from throughout the travelling community turning up on a biting cold day to pay their last respects. People travelled from all over Britain, Europe, America and Ireland to line the streets leading to St Mary's RC Church.

Among them were all of the 100 residents still living on Mellishaw. They held an all night vigil before leaving early to make the journey across the country to

Mellishaw Caravan Park.

Stockton. Many of them were to move away from Morecambe over the following months, unable to stay at the spot where one of their number had been so brutally taken.

Maga's body was carried in a Mercedes hearse, her mahogany coffin adorned with a cross-shaped wreath of yellow orchids and red carnations. Attached was the simple message, "To our precious daughter. You'll always be loved. Good night. God Bless. Mam, Dad, Jimmy and Joe." The funeral cortege stretched out for more than one mile with 136 cars and vans crawling through the streets in silent convoy.

The travellers upheld their tradition of allowing the women to go into church while the menfolk waited outside as Maga's brass-handled coffin was carried shoulder high into the church as her family shuffled in behind. Three flat-back trucks had to be used to carry the hundreds of floral tributes in every shape and size to a much-loved child whose death had shocked the nation.

Father Michael Corbett conducted the Mass of the Angels, accompanied by hymns especially chosen by Carol: *The Lord's My Shepherd*, *How Great Thou Art*, *Be Still And Know I Am With You* and *Abide With Me*. During the service Father Corbett spoke movingly of a "loving and trusting child" and praised the Lowthers for their dignity in the face of such an awful tragedy.

He had made daily visits to comfort the family in the weeks before the funeral service and grew to know them well. Sister Anna, a nun from Sheffield known throughout the travelling community for her pastoral work, also made a reading.

After the service, the youngster's coffin was taken the two miles to Oxbridge Lane Cemetery and laid to rest on a bed of daffodils alongside her grandfather Joe.

Johnston went on trial at Preston Crown Court on January 18, 1989. Maga's family were there to see justice done and as the teenager was brought into the court dwarfed by three police officers, the little girl's distraught father James made a lunge from the public gallery for the dock before he was restrained by officers.

> **❝ ...the little girl's distraught father James made a lunge from the public gallery... ❞**

As the hearing got underway the prosecutor outlined what he described as the "quite appalling and horrible" facts of the case. Throughout the six-day trial Johnston maintained his pretence that he was not responsible for killing his cousin and that the mystery man he claimed he had spotted by the tip fire had carried out the attack. At one point James Lowther broke down in the witness box as he described the last time he saw his daughter alive. As he finished his testimony he turned to Johnston and screamed, "You're dead... you're dead."

The centre piece of the prosecution's case provided a landmark in the Lancashire justice system. The use of DNA evidence was still in its infancy at the time, but the jury was told tests on Maga's body and her discarded clothes found there was only a one in 34.5 million chance that someone other than Johnston had been responsible for the attack. It was the first time genetic fingerprinting had been used in the county's courts.

The jury of ten men and two women spent a night in a hotel after they failed to reach a unanimous verdict. The following day they resumed their deliberations and the judge told them he would accept a majority verdict. After a total of five and a half hours considering the overwhelming evidence lined up against Johnston, they returned to the courtroom to deliver a majority 11-1 guilty verdict.

Friends and relatives clapped and cheered as the guilty verdict was returned. Johnston showed no emotion as the judge Sir Sanderson Temple QC ordered him to stand and told him, "You have been convicted of a murder in circumstances which were revolting, appalling in the extreme and abominable."

He ordered the child killer be detained at Her Majesty's Pleasure with a recommendation he serve at least 14 years behind bars and he was led away to boos and jeers from 30 relatives in the public gallery.

Detective Superintendent Bill Hacking is now retired but has vivid memories of the case. In 2008 he told the *Evening Post*, "It was really, really horrific. Of my 38 years in the force it was the worst child murder I had ever seen. It always surprised me the case didn't seem to provoke as much public outcry as I expected. People were up in arms about it but it seemed to be quickly forgotten, unlike more recent child murders like the Soham case and Jamie Bulger."

Johnston served his sentence in HMP Magheraberry, in Northern Ireland, and was released in 2004 despite Carol's battle to keep him locked up. She handed in a 3,000-name petition to Downing Street and a letter of protest to officials at the province's Stormont House as she carried out a lone protest outside Magheraberry, to no avail.

Speaking to the *Lancashire Evening Post* on the 20th anniversary of her daughter's murder Carol revealed she has dressed in black and been on anti-depressant tablets since Maga's death. She has turned her back on the travellers' lifestyle and lives in a terraced house near to her daughter's grave which she tends to every day.

She said, "The first few years after she died I bought presents and left them there for her. I bought prams and dolls and they were all taken away but I didn't care. I used to take the children there with a picnic blanket when they were small and stay with her for the day."

"Every year I still buy her a battery operated Christmas tree with lights because she loved Christmas and I light it up until the New Year for her. Maga never died in my heart – she was always there."

"I wake up in the morning with Maga on my mind and go to sleep with her."

"I cry a lot and still have nightmares. I dream I have found Maga and that I have her at the foot of my bed and when I wake up she's gone. I dream she's in hospital with tubes coming out of her with her eyes half open and the doctors are telling me to talk to her, that she's going to live. This will never end for me."

❝ This will never end for me. ❞

"I still feel like when it's raining she's getting wet, and when it's snowing the ice and snow are laying on top of her. When it's frosty and you can hear your feet crunching on the ground, I think I've left her in the cold."

"I keep thinking my Maga's crying for me."

CHAPTER EIGHT

Evil in the playing fields

Annette Wade, Carleton, Blackpool, July 18, 1989

AS he climbed up the drainpipe outside the corner shop, John Heeley was unaware he was being watched. Silently he squeezed through an open window and into the flat above Ted's grocers. The elderly neighbour who had spotted him quickly dialled 999. Inside the flat shopkeeper Graham Elliott was asleep with his wife Kerry and their young son Gary.

Heeley crept across the room and stole two keys before slipping downstairs and letting himself out.

Police were already waiting for him at the door. He was arrested and within hours appeared in court, where he was remanded in custody for five days. At his next appearance he was granted bail on the condition he remained at his lodgings and kept a night-time curfew.

Ted's grocers shop was just 30 yards from Heeley's digs in Caunce Street, in the back streets of Blackpool. The petty criminal was brought up in the resort and, no matter where work took him, he would inevitably gravitate back to the town. With its cheap rooms and ask-no-questions casual labour, it was the ideal world for the itinerant worker on the fringes of society.

After completing an 18 month sentence in Hull Prison for robbery, Heeley moved back to Blackpool late in 1988 where he became a voluntary patient in the psychiatric unit at Blackpool Victoria Hospital. He drifted between a number of bedsits and guesthouses and, by May 1989, was renting a room in Laurence and Mary Sherry's terraced house opposite the Victory pub in Caunce Street.

It was a warm summer and he would spend his days stripped to the waist perched in the

156 Caunce Street, Blackpool, Heeley's former home.

sunshine on the Sherrys' garden wall, or sat on a roadside bench outside nearby St Thomas's Parish Church watching, winking and whistling as the young girls left Devonshire Road School.

John Heeley.

With his long hair, tattoos and army trousers he stuck out a like sore thumb as he strutted around the area swinging a long chain from his waistband bearing keys and a knife. Some of the children were terrified. Others thought him a bit of a joke and would shout "Rambo" at him before running away. Heeley often bought sweets for the local children in Ted's corner shop and would loiter around the children's play area near the high-rise flats at Layton.

After the break-in at the shop, police searched his room and discovered knives, an axe and a Samurai sword. He was kicked out of his lodgings and took to sleeping in a squat in a derelict house a few doors up from the Sherrys. He continued to hang around Caunce Street, often calling in at the Victory pub for a half a lager. Few regulars at the pub ever spoke to Heeley but they nicknamed him Johnny Comanche because of his habit of wearing feathers tucked into a white headband.

It was a nickname he revelled in, as those who did speak to him would find out. Heeley was always ready to regale anyone who would listen with his fanciful tales of how he was a Red Indian of Canadian descent through his mother from the famous Chief Cochise. He believed he embodied the soul of a North American brave whose land was stolen by the white settlers. He talked of returning to Canada to join his tribe to carry on the fight. On other days he would tell how his blood type proved he was related to both Japanese and British Royal families. His father was, he would claim, the son of the late Duke of Windsor.

> **❝ ...police searched his room and discovered knives, an axe and a Samurai sword. ❞**

To the parents who lived around Caunce Street, he was far from nobility – they believed he was a pervert with a fixation on under age girls. They would complain about Heeley making improper remarks to their children and, on three separate occasions, he attempted to entice one nine-year-old girl to his room to watch pornographic videos with him. The youngster was approached just yards from her home in nearby Addison Crescent and only the quick thinking actions of her 12-year-old brother stopped her from going off with Heeley after he jumped in to drag his sister away.

By July 3 people living in the neighbourhood had endured enough of his bizarre and menacing behaviour. He followed a 13-year-old girl home from school. Terrified, she ducked into a telephone box and pretended to call the police. Heeley walked away but enough was enough and a group of the local parents went to confront the 30-year-old. As they attempted to remonstrate with him, Heeley swung at them with a baseball bat and the parents fled to Ted's and barricaded themselves inside as he ranted and raved on the pavement.

The police were called and he was arrested again.

The following day he appeared in court on a charge of possessing an offensive weapon and was remanded in custody. Two days later he was freed on bail and a court date set for July 13. But it would not be that long before his next brush with the law.

His third arrest came on July 9 when one of the local mothers saw him sitting on a bench next to an eight-year-old girl. He had his arm around her and was talking to two young boys on a bicycle. The police picked him up, brought him back to the street and asked some of the mothers to identify him. Many refused to leave their homes to help for fear Heeley would spot them. He was hauled before magistrates the following day and accused of conduct likely to cause a breach of the peace and of threatening behaviour.

Police asked the Crown Prosecution Service to oppose any application for bail, but technically he could not be held because conviction of neither offence carried a custodial sentence. He was locked up for 24 hours for more legal discussion, then, on July 11, sent to live in a bail hostel in Blackburn.

Two days later he went missing.

Annette Wade was excited. It was the last few days of term and ahead lay six long weeks of summer holidays. This summer she had made a new friend to play with in the fields close to the family home in Blackpool Old Road, Poulton.

Annette's parents, Mary and Brian Wade, face the media at Lancashire Police press conference.

Brian and Mary Wade had moved to the semi-detached house seven months earlier so their only daughter would be safer. Concerned about bringing up a child in a flat on a busy main road, they did not like letting Annette out to play unsupervised. The move to Carleton with its views across open fields eased their fears and in the hot sunny evenings after school, the popular nine-year-old would head out to play with her pals. Her parents bought their daughter a watch which beeped on the hour so Annette would not lose track of time as she played out.

Known as a bit of a tomboy, whatever the weather she loved the new found freedom of playing outdoors on her beloved BMX bicycle and racing around the playground on neighbouring Cottam Hall playing fields. It was on the playing fields that Annette met John Heeley.

He had been living rough in the fields behind her home since failing to return to the bail hostel in Blackburn a few days earlier. Annette was playing on the swings, with her bike lying on the floor beside her, when she first met Heeley. Dressed all in black and drinking from a bottle, he sat down on the grass about ten yards away and starting talking to the youngster.

Before long she jumped down from the swing and went to sit with Heeley, and the two chatted away as he boasted of his Red Indian ancestry and royal blood until two of her friends arrived and she went back to playing on the swings with her shoulder length hair dancing in the breeze. Larking about, Annette stood up on the swing and fell off. Although unhurt she grabbed her bike and cycled home leaving Heeley still sat on the grass. In those few minutes, they had spent talking he had already tricked his way into the little girl's confidence and, over the space of a few days, they would meet up after school. Heeley even gave her three 20p coins which she later told her mother had been given to her by a friend. It was her little secret. The trusting youngster returned the favour, giving her new friend a present of her own, the gold coloured cloth bag in which she kept her recorder.

Word of Heeley's den and the strange looking man who lived there with the feather in his headband quickly spread among local children. Curious to get a look at this mysterious figure who looked like a Red Indian and lived like Huckleberry Finn, they would sneak into the field to spy on him. Watching from a distance, they would look for the plume of smoke from his campfire as the former Territorial Army soldier prepared his meals. Then the braver ones would creep closer for a better look.

His makeshift den was constructed from a blue blanket stretched on a rope between two trees like a tent. Underneath it lay an orange and brown sleeping bag. The tail feathers of a bird had been nailed to a fence nearby. The spot nestled between two dense hedges which met at the top to form a tunnel forming a natural hide. One 11-year-old later recalled, "We came across his den and we saw a man playing with a knife. We were scared but excited too – it was like an adventure. We ran away but later we went back and spoke to him. He seemed quite nice at first but told us to watch out because the farmer would get him in trouble if he was found. Later we saw a man walking his dog nearby so we ran back and warned him. We knew it was all a big secret and that he should not be there."

It was not just the children who took notice of the newcomer living in the fields. With his strange outlaw clothes, scruffy appearance and wild staring eyes, he stood out in the quiet Carleton community. During the few days he was camped out he would make daily visits to fill up his containers with water at nearby Carleton Crematorium. He was the talk of the neighbourhood as he called in to the local Post Office to stock up on Pot Noodles, Mars bars and cigarettes. And most of the talk was of the menace the brooding stranger exuded. Much as he did a couple of miles away in Caunce Street, Heeley spent his time watching children in the playground on Cottam Hall. Attempting to lure one group of three 14-year-old girls with a thick wad of money, he told them he was the descendant of a

> **" He was the talk of the neighbourhood... "**

Scottish king and that his mother was Spanish. He told another teenager he was only there to watch the girls' legs as they played netball. Unnerved, they made their excuses and got up to walk away. Heeley merely replied, "It's nice meeting you, I hope to meet you again sometime."

But to Annette, the friendly hobo Heeley was her secret friend and she did not breathe a word about him to her classmates at Breck Primary School.

On Tuesday, July 18, the night before school broke up for the summer, Brian and Mary Wade picked up their daughter from the school gates at 3.15pm. Brian had just finished work as a line manager on the 6am to 2pm shift at Symbol Biscuits factory in Blackpool. When they arrived home Annette raced into her bedroom and changed out of her school uniform into a T-shirt, Bermuda shorts and white socks. Proudly pinned on her T-shirt was a badge with 'Don't talk to strangers' emblazoned across it. She came downstairs and asked her mum to tell her when it was 4pm.

But Annette couldn't wait. A few minutes later, at 3.55pm, she left the house telling her parents she was off to play with her friend Aaran who lived opposite. Brian watched his beloved daughter cross the road. It was the last time he saw her alive. Instead of going to Aaran's house, Annette cycled to Cottam Hall playing fields to keep her pre-arranged meeting in the summer sunshine with John Heeley.

Earlier in the day her pals asked her out to play after tea but Annette said she had a 'special meeting' and gave nothing else away. That afternoon Heeley had offered to show the schoolgirl his den and the temptation was too much. If Annette was excited about her secret meeting, then Heeley also spent the day preparing for their rendezvous.

At lunchtime he walked into Poulton to get his hair cut at Peter J's salon. As assistant Jacqueline Saunders washed his long hair, Heeley attempted to chat her up and asked her to meet him for a drink later. Then he joked with hairdresser Linda Brown that she had not made him look rough enough. She laughed back that he did not have enough hair left to do anything with. Shorn of his Rambo locks, he

143

was clearly in high spirits. After having his trim he paid the £4.50 bill from the big roll of notes he had flashed to the girls in the park. Next he posed for photographs in a photo machine before heading to the village Post Office where he bought a temporary passport for £7.50, telling post mistress Doreen Thompson he was planning a trip to France. Preparations made, he picked up some fizzy pop, beer and chocolate and strolled back to the playing fields where he spent the rest of the afternoon lazing in the sunshine. And waiting.

Cottam Hall playing fields was linked to Woodhouse Farm by a tunnel formed where a dyke passed beneath the Blackpool to Preston railway line. When Annette caught up with Heeley at the swings they chatted for a while then walked together from the playground and off through the tunnel towards the farmer's fields, the youngster wheeling her red BMX by her side.

At 4.35pm David Boardman was walking in the fields when he heard a muted scream. Looking around he saw no-one and, thinking it was a child playing, continued on his way.

Forty minutes later two anglers arrived at a pond behind Woodhouse Farm to spend the evening fishing but were distracted by smoke rising from the far side of the field known locally as Goose Meadow. As they strained to see the source, the pair heard a bang and caught a fleeting glance of a man with a bag climbing through the hedgerow into the adjacent field.

With Lancashire in the grip of a warm dry spell the men were concerned the flames could spread and went over to investigate. By the time they arrived at the fire all the anglers could see through the thick smoke was what appeared to be a pile of burning clothes and a bicycle. The noise they had heard was the sound of a tyre exploding in the flames.

They decided to alert the farmer, Bob Aspden. He quickly filled a milk churn with water, loaded it on to his tractor and started up the vehicle for the 300-yard journey to the remote corner of his land where the fire was still billowing out smoke.

At the scene he realised the hedgerow was not alight and there appeared to be a pile about two feet high ablaze on the nearby path. He filled a bucket from the milk churn and extinguished the fire.

Once the smoke cleared, Mr Aspden removed the bicycle from the top of the remains and saw a large pile of twigs and leaves. As he pulled sticks away he was confronted by a horrific sight.

> **“** As he pulled sticks away he was confronted by a horrific sight. **”**

Underneath the pile lay the charred and mutilated body of a child.

Annette Wade had been raped and then stabbed three times in the neck and once in the chest. She was just half a mile from her home.

Unable to comprehend what he saw Mr Aspden returned to the farmhouse to get his wife Margaret who called the police. The scene was sealed off and detectives quickly found a den hidden between the hedges. Inside was a Calor gas cylinder and barbecue stolen from the Aspdens' farmhouse, empty tins and bottles along with hen's feathers and lighter fuel.

But the killer was already miles away.

Tattooed killer John Heeley.

John Heeley was born on May 9, 1959, in his grandmother's home at Clowne, Derbyshire. One of 18 children, his parents separated before he was born and he was fostered as a baby. He later went back to his natural mother but from an early age he was deemed completely out of control and found mixing with other children difficult.

He was constantly in trouble and by the age of five was taken into care. He later returned home for short periods and the family moved to Manchester after Heeley burned down a haystack in Clowne. By the time he was 10 years old Heeley was back in care and he lived in various children's homes in the Blackpool area until he was 18. His first serious brush with the law came at the age of 11 when he appeared before the juvenile bench at Lytham magistrates court to faces charges of breaking into holiday chalets. He was handed a conditional discharge.
At the time he was a pupil at Warbreck High School but was moved to Red Bank

approved school, and over the following two years made five more appearances in court on theft and burglary charges, before being moved to a special school in Cumbria. Over the next few years Heeley notched up more than 20 court appearances mainly for burglaries and attempted burglaries.

In 1978 he was jailed for eight months at Preston Crown Court for stealing cash from a 16-year-old boy at knifepoint. On his release Heeley moved to London where he met Linda Francis in a pub in Croydon where he had a job as a builder. The couple wed but the marriage broke up within a year. She later recalled, "I really didn't know him until we married, but then discovered he was a loony with a split personality. He beat me with his fists until I had to leave."

By the time he ended up back in Blackpool for the last time, he had served three jail terms and a total of four years and nine months behind bars, but none was for anything as serious as rape and murder.

The burning of Annette Wade's body on a bonfire was not just a means of covering up the evidence of his wicked crime. After killing the youngster he wrapped her lifeless body in a makeshift funeral shroud made from a piece of blue curtain. In Heeley's warped mind he was carrying out the traditional Red Indian funeral by cremating his dead on a burning pyre. He covered her remains with twigs and doused them with petrol before setting them alight. Then the next stage of his evil plan kicked in.

Two nights earlier, as pensioner Grace May slept in her bungalow in Thirlmere Avenue, Poulton, Heeley forced his way in through a window and stole cash, jewellery and the keys to her Mini Metro City. He pushed the car off the driveway and out of the cul-de-sac before starting up the engine. A short while later he left the metallic green car in a residents' car park a few hundred yards away in Sherbourne Court, Carleton. The innocuous Metro was to be his getaway car. Fleeing across the fields, he headed for Sherbourne Close.

But at the very time he was disposing of Annette Wade's lifeless body, an elderly resident from the flats in Sherbourne Court, Joan Bennetts, called the police, concerned at the strange car which had been parked outside their home for two days.

It was 5.15pm and two officers arrived to check out the Metro. They confirmed it was stolen and locked its doors before leaving it for a fingerprint expert to return

Aerial view of the murder scene in farmland on the edge of Carleton, Blackpool.

later. Having discovered who the car belonged to, Mrs Bennetts went to telephone Mrs May to let her know her vehicle was safe. She had only bought it one week before and relied on a car to get her around.

As she put down the telephone, Mrs Bennetts looked out of the window and saw an unkempt figure unlock the car boot and put a bedroll and two rucksacks inside. She rushed outside and up to the car window and bravely shouted, "Get out, that is not your car."

Heeley stared back and replied, "Yes it is. See I have the keys," before driving off. Police had missed the man, who by sunset would become Britain's most wanted criminal, by minutes. As Heeley left Carleton he was in no hurry to get out of Blackpool.

While police arrived at his den to launch a murder inquiry he was in the Stanley Arms pub in the resort having a pint of bitter. The killer then called on a friend to show off his new car, telling her he had bought it that day for £800. Heeley asked her if she fancied going for a drink and spending the night in the car with him. She declined and the two went to a café instead for milkshake and toast before he finally took to the road to make his escape.

He hit the M6 at 10pm, and later picked up hitchhiker David Turner in the stolen Metro at Keele service station. Carrying on his journey south he stopped at

Toddington services to fill up the car with fuel but instead of using petrol he filled up the tank with diesel.

The car carried on for a few more miles before inevitably breaking down in Swiss Cottage, north London. Heeley abandoned the Metro in a bus lane on the Finchley Road, bade farewell to Turner and melted into the night.

Detectives quickly realised the link between the scruffy vagrant, the stolen Mini Metro and the horrific murder of a nine-year-old girl on a sunny summer's evening.

By 8pm Brian and Mary Wade were worried that Annette had not returned home and as Mr Wade drove around the district, his wife contacted the police. Detectives quickly drew the heart breaking link between the horrific events just half a mile away and the Wades' anguished telephone call. Unable to speak to officers, a distraught Brian was taken to Layton mortuary to identify his precious daughter's body.

A police officer stands guard near to the murder scene.

The following morning at 8am, the Metro was discovered in London and a parking ticket slapped on the windscreen. Within minutes of inputting the vehicle's registration number B970WBV into police computers its significance was realised and the car was sealed off.

At Breck School headteacher Frank Tyas broke the dreadful news to Annette's friends at a special assembly. He told the *Lancashire Evening Post*, "I don't think any parents in Poulton will be letting their children out tonight. Since joining us last September, Annette has been a friendly, popular member of our school community with a cheerful smile for everybody. We all miss her very much." At the school gates mothers clutched their children close as they sobbed in small groups, numb and unable to comprehend the horror which had struck in their midst. Mother-of-three Marion Herbert summed up their feelings, "What sort of world is this? When innocent children can't play in peace – as we used to when we were children – for fear of being picked off, like prey, by evil men and women."

Forensic examination of tins of soup, Coca Cola cans and other items found in the ditch close to where Annette's body was found revealed Heeley's fingerprints. Detectives had their number one suspect and on July 20 took the unusual step of publicly naming John Geoffrey Heeley, also known as John Geoffrey Higham, as the man they wanted to interview.

The rare move followed discussions between senior detectives and John Bates, chief crown prosecutor for Lancashire and Cumbria, about the possible legal repercussions. It was agreed there could be no contempt of court because a warrant had not yet been issued for Heeley's arrest. But legal experts were conscious that after his arrest, Heeley might claim the release of his name would prejudice his chance of a fair trial.

Det Supt John Ashton, the man who led the murder investigation, told reporters, "We have the right to release a suspect's name if it is in the public interest, and this most certainly was. What would people have said if we had not released it and he had murdered someone else?"

It was a genuine fear. Det Supt Ashton later explained, "I acted in the public interest and could not take the chance of another child being perhaps badly injured or indeed killed. Had something tragic happened and I had not taken that course of action I would never have forgiven myself."

Details of the tattoos which covered his arms and torso were provided and a police mug shot sent out to newsrooms across the land. By teatime Heeley's face was on all of the national television bulletins and the front pages of the region's newspapers. The wild-eyed Rambo was now Britain's most wanted man.

> **" The wild-eyed Rambo was now Britain's most wanted man. "**

A surveillance operation was mounted at Blackpool magistrates court where Heeley was due to appear on the charges which mounted up against him in the weeks before Annette's murder. The break-in at Ted's cornershop; the baseball attack on the parents sick of his perverted behaviour; and his improper approaches to a schoolgirl. Unsurprisingly he failed to turn up.

People living in the shell-shocked community of Poulton inundated the incident room in Fleetwood with sightings of the scruffy Red Indian who had stalked their streets in recent days. Det Supt Ashton assembled a 50-strong murder team to sift through the evidence pouring in.

At a press conference held at Fleetwood Police Station he said, "I am deeply saddened and don't know how one describes a person who can perpetrate this kind of offence on a trusting, loving child of nine who is just setting out in her life. I don't know how they would have felt had they seen the reaction of Annette's parents. Every policeman in Britain is now looking for the man who committed this evil crime."

The man he was talking about had already fled the country. After dumping the Metro, Heeley made his way into central London and on to Victoria Station where he caught a direct train to Dover. Once at the coastal port he gave his own name, paid £12 for a day ticket to Boulogne and boarded the 12.30pm ferry bound for France. After he crossed the Channel, the killer hitched a lift to Marseilles with a lorry driver. But detectives were already on to him. His idle small talk with the postmistress Doreen Thompson as he paid for his temporary passport was quickly identified as a crucial lead.

An all ports warning was issued across all cross-Channel ferry terminals. Detectives believed the child killer was on his way to see an ex-girlfriend in the Versailles area of Paris. Checks were made on passenger lists and Heeley's name was confirmed as a traveller. Lancashire Police alerted New Scotland Yard and Interpol.

Five thousand posters in English and French were produced bearing Heeley's photograph and details. Appeals were made to British lorry drivers and holidaymakers heading over the Channel at the start of the school break to keep an eye out for Heeley, and a warrant for his arrest was issued. Detectives and legal experts decided a warrant was of paramount importance, because under French law a suspect can only be kept for four hours and in theory Heeley could have been released before Lancashire officers arrived if there was no warrant.

On Friday Annette's shattered parents bravely agreed to speak to the media. Choking back tears and clutching her daughter's favourite white teddy bear Snowy, Mary, 41, said, "The bottom has just dropped out of our lives. It's hard to describe how we feel. Words just fail and I still sit at the window waiting for her to come across the road on her bike.

"When we came to the house and she was allowed outside she was in her element. She could then play with her friends whenever she liked and loved the freedom. She had so many friends she would go round to them all but if she was playing, even round the corner, she would always tell us where she was going.

"If anyone knows where this man is, this maniac, whatever he is, they should report it to the police. The sooner the police can get hold of this man, the sooner my daughter can be laid to rest."

Her 40-year-old husband Brian added, "We want to get back to a normal life somehow, but I don't know how."

Eight days after the murder and seven days after the last confirmed sighting of the murderer, there was a dramatic breakthrough. Two Special Branch officers from Kent Police were monitoring passengers returning to Dover, looking for suspected drug runners, when they spotted Heeley stepping off P&O Ferries' *Pride of Hythe* after it docked at 3pm from Boulogne. The officers recognised his face from photographs and watched as he went through immigration at the port's Eastern Dock Terminal before pouncing. He was arrested, stripped and his clothes sent away for forensic examination.

Handcuffed, the sadistic child killer went quietly and without any fuss telling officers, "I have been in France for two weeks and this has ruined my holiday." Dressed in a police regulation white boiler suit, Heeley was transferred to Ladywell police station in Dover, where he spent the night behind bars. Items in his possession were linked to the murder scene, including Annette's gold coloured recorder bag. But there was no sign of the murder weapon. Det Supt Ashton and other officers travelled down to Dover to bring Heeley back to

❝ But there was no sign of the murder weapon. ❞

Fleetwood for questioning. For 300 miles, all the way from Kent to a police cell in Lancashire, he stared through the car window and barely said a word as their van, flanked by a police escort, sped north. His silence suited detectives. Under strict regulation surrounding suspects, the clock starts ticking with the first question and they wanted Heeley back on their manor before beginning their interview.

When he arrived in Lancashire, officers decided to change tack and take him to Blackpool police station to avoid an angry crowd of people gathered outside

Heeley returned to the crime scene during his trial.

Fleetwood police station, some of whom had waited for hours to glimpse the evil killer. There he was interviewed for three hours and refused to say a word. It was a pattern he maintained over the following days as he kept up a stony silence.

Ten days after Annette Wade was brutally knifed to death Heeley appeared before Fleetwood magistrates court handcuffed to a police officer and flanked by three other officers. Once again a large crowd was waiting outside the court building.

During a five-minute hearing he was charged with the schoolgirl's murder. His solicitor Andrew Greensmith took the unusual step of asking for reporting restrictions surrounding the case to be lifted. Throughout his many arrests down the years for petty offences, the pattern had always been the same as Heeley steadfastly refused to admit any guilt. One solicitor who previously represented him explained, "He was caught with a penknife he had taken from a Preston shop by the store detective. It was in his pocket with the price still on it. Time after time he said he hadn't done it. He just sat there for 30 minutes denying the obvious. Then he went back to the cells saying he had sacked me. I wasn't unhappy being sacked by him. He has got mad staring eyes."

This time he faced a murder charge but Heeley had already formulated an alibi. Magistrates were told he had spent the day of Annette's murder at Blackpool Pleasure Beach. While strolling around the theme park he recalled seeing a tourist with a video camera and believed he may have been caught on film. It was a hopeless lie but he appealed for the mystery cameraman to come forward and exonerate him. No-one emerged to support his story, but it was one he would stick to until the moment he was convicted.

On August 16, family and friends packed into the small chapel at Carleton crematorium to say their final farewells to the child that had been violently snatched from their lives. Police officers lined the route from her home in Blackpool Old Road through Blackpool Road and Stocks Lane to the crematorium. Senior officers from across the resort joined mourners as the vicar of St Chad's Church in Poulton, Canon Carl Berryman, led the service. Scores of floral tributes filled the chapel, including one spelling out ANNETTE in white flowers from regulars and staff at The Falcon pub and a wreath from Lancashire Police. Two white teddy bears made out of flowers were created in memory of Annette's beloved teddy bear Snowy.

Canon Berryman described Annette as a, "lively, loving, outgoing little girl" with a ready smile and a trusting nature. The whole community had learned of her death with great sadness and shock, he said, and was united in their support and sympathy for Annette's family in the "dark weeks and months ahead."

He paid tribute to the short life of "just a normal, little girl" who had touched the hearts of so many. "No-one can ever take those short years away from you because they are there in your heart. She is always with you."

Outside, as if on cue, the sun passed behind a bank of clouds and the heavens opened, raindrops mingling freely with the teardrops of mourners young and old gathered at Annette's graveside just a few hundred yards from where she was murdered.

On April 25, 1990, John Heeley went on trial at Liverpool Crown Court. A succession of witnesses described the stranger dressed like a Red Indian who appeared in the small Carleton community the previous summer and now stood in the dock before them.

The jury of six men and six women learned of a piece of blue curtain found wrapped around Annette's body which matched material found in the squat in

Evening Post

31,795 WEDNESDAY, JULY 19, 1989   TOWN & COUNTY – NORTH   19p

Abducted, assaulted, murdered – what sort of man could do this to a little girl?

ANNETTE: THE KILLING FIELD

Caunce Street where Heeley told detectives he was living. Knife marks on the curtain matched knife marks on Annette's T-shirt.

They were told of distinctive striped trousers, Doc Marten boots and blue jeans with a Union Jack patch which locals remember him wearing – all discovered in a den by the funeral pyre lit to destroy Annette's body. Old Holborn tobacco, which the accused habitually smoked, tins and bottles with his fingerprints and DNA stains on his clothes were all found at the scene and all pointed squarely to Heeley as the killer. The passport, the stolen Mini Metro, the tattoos, feathered headband and six-inch knife, the fistful of gold rings, stocky 5ft 7ins frame and wild, staring, deep-set eyes. He was the man in the wanted photographs in every newspaper in the land.

But still he stuck to his alibi. He had been at the Pleasure Beach, he had bought a beef burger there from a stall, he had been seen by two friends and strayed on to a holidaymaker's video outside the Gold Mine ride.

The court heard of sightings of a man chatting with a young girl in Cottam Hall playing fields in the days before her murder. One grandmother described how she felt uneasy as she watched them by the swings and kept her eyes on them for some time to ensure the child was alright. The witness, Margaret Murray, told the court, "My husband and I discussed what we had seen. The girl was very young. We decided to sit on a bench to keep them in our view.

"We wanted to keep an eye on them. We did not like the look of him. We felt it was our duty to keep an eye on her. We made up our mind together to sit there and look to see what happened. We agreed that if they got up together we would go over and make some pretext about asking the girl where she was going.

"It was difficult. The man might have been a relative, but we decided we must still sit here and see the girl was alright. My husband and I felt happier when she peddled away.

Mrs Murray later identified the man as Heeley and the girl as Annette.

Midway through the trial the judge, jury, lawyers and court staff were transported by coach on the 120-mile round trip to Carleton to see for themselves the fields where Annette was killed. Handcuffed between two prison guards, Heeley was taken to the scene of his awful crime in a prison van.

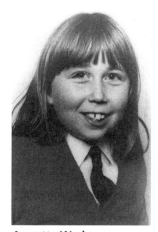

Annette Wade.

The visit was like nothing the village of Carleton had ever seen before, yet the residents seemed to want no reminder of the horror Heeley brought to their streets nine months earlier. Not a curtain twitched and the streets were virtually empty as the jury arrived. More than 20 uniformed police officers were dotted around the village and the entrance to Woodhouse Farm was shut off.

The whole courtroom cast was driven past the cordon and into the farm grounds. A detective guided the procession a quarter of a mile to the ditch where Annette's body was discovered on a smouldering bonfire. The 12 men and women stopped at the spot where the little girl was butchered and bowed their heads as they joined together to say a quiet prayer. The thicket had long been cleared away by the farmer and, with it, Heeley's den.

As they travelled around the quiet neighbourhood, the detective pointed out seven different locations jurors had heard described over the previous two weeks inside the panelled walls of Liverpool Crown Court. They returned to hear Heeley argue all 39 witnesses who had seen him around Carleton were mistaken and there was a "mimic" at large.

He had never lived in a den in the far corner of Woodhouse Farm's fields. Police had planted items with his fingerprints in the den. He had bought the recorder bag from a second hand shop to sheath his knife. The blue curtain with the knife marks on it in the squat was his, but it was a remarkable coincidence that a section of the same material should be found wrapped around the dead schoolgirl. He had never met Annette Wade. He was, he said, "No psychopath."

The jury did not believe him.

At the end of a three-week trial, they took less than two hours to find John Heeley guilty of murder. As he sat impassively in the dock with his arms folded, Mr Justice Kennedy told him, "You have been convicted on overwhelming evidence of murdering a nine-year-old child. Even if it were not compulsory for me to do so I would have no hesitation in sentencing you to imprisonment for life."

Brian Wade attended every day of the trial of the man who so cruelly took his daughter's life. He was forced to endure her killer pulling his tongue out at him from the dock and staring at him across the courtroom until a screen was erected between them.

Speaking after the hearing he told the *Lancashire Evening Post*, "What I thought of him could not be printed. I admit being there wasn't easy but it was just something I felt I had to do. I had to see it through. I wanted to come here every day to hear it for myself. I said right at the start that I would see this through.

"Certain things bring everything back, the little everyday things in life. It's worse if you've nothing on your mind or you're doing nothing, just sitting there thinking about what we'd be doing if Annette was alive, like picking her up from school.

"I would say he should hang. The do-gooders always try to prevent the death sentence being brought back. But I am sure if something similar happened to them they would change their minds."

Mary added, "There is no doubt about it; if it is proved that a person has committed a crime for an offence like this, he should hang."

❝ I would say he should hang. ❞

Five months after Heeley was convicted of murdering their daughter, Brian and Mary Wade gave birth to a baby boy.

CHAPTER NINE

The Curse of Withnell Villa

David Wilson, Withnell, near Chorley, March 5, 1992

MICHELLE Wilson flicked on the television and curled up on the sofa for a night in front of the box. She had just waved off the rest of the family who were driving to her younger sister Lisa's new home in School Lane, Brinscall, near Chorley, to help lay a carpet. With mum Barbara, dad David, and Lisa's fiancé Mark Stephenson all going along, Michelle, 26, figured that joining them would just be a case of too many cooks. After a busy day fielding telephone calls and juggling figures at the accountants' office in Darwen where she worked as her dad's personal assistant, all she wanted was to put her feet up.

At 8.45pm, there was a knock at the door. Nothing unusual about that, she thought. After all, the Wilson household was a busy family home – and anyway, dad's foreign friends had been visiting recently. Moments later Michelle Wilson knew that these were no friends. She opened the door to find herself staring down the barrel of a gun and though she fought desperately to shut them out, one of the family's dutiful Labrador dogs, eager to protect Michelle from harm, got in the way and her two masked attackers were soon inside.

Under the yellow glare of the kitchen lights Michelle met them eye-to-eye. The first man, the one in charge, was small and wiry – maybe 5ft 6ins – and wearing a short-length car coat. His black, woollen single-slit balaclava made him every inch the mercenary... and so did the silencer on the handgun he was wielding in her direction. The second man was thicker-set but wearing an identical mask and cradling a similarly ugly handgun in black gloved hands. Hidden beneath his black canvas bomber jacket, a knife in a brown leather sheath.

Trying to keep calm Michelle could only say, "don't hurt me." As the shorter of the gunmen took her by the hand, she fought back tears and managed to add a terrified, "What do you want?"

In a menacing, mock Irish accent he told her, "Your dad knows what we want. It's about some money from a few years ago. I want to know how he invested it. It seems he's been down to London to see the Fraud Squad."

Michelle's mind was reeling. She had worked closely with her father, she had even acted as a cash courier in certain transatlantic deals, and she knew he moved in the big league. She also knew that despite the twin Mercedes in the driveway of their secluded farmhouse, named Withnell Villa, her dad was teetering on the verge of bankruptcy with huge debts.

But guns? In the quiet Lancashire village of Withnell?

As she struggled to make some sense out of what was happening, the thinner of the gunmen taped her hands behind her back and dragged her upstairs with the chilling words, "Come on...I want you to show me the bedroom." His intentions were all too clear. But another of the family's dogs, snarling and barking at the top of the stairs, forced the gunman to think again. The next two hours were the longest of her life.

At 11.10pm a car pulled into the drive. The stocky gunman grabbed Michelle's arm, forced her into the kitchen and silently pointed to the open safety catch on his pistol – one wrong move and she was dead. The front door was locked. David Wilson rapped on the door, shouting, "Come on Michelle, open the door!"

> **" ...one wrong move and she was dead. "**

At gunpoint his daughter replied vaguely, "You'll have to come the other way because I can't get there." The 47-year-old smiled. He thought his eldest daughter was fooling around; she'd probably got too comfortable in front of the TV. But he was wrong, very wrong. Entering through the side door, the family took in the horror of the situation.

Michelle bound at gunpoint, and a second weapon trained on them.

"Get in," ordered one of the men, "she's not been harmed." Lisa screamed hysterically with incomprehension and fear. David Wilson kept calm. But he knew.

He knew about the Mexican Colonel Hector Portillo – the man with whom he had arranged to ship millions of dollars of cigarettes. He knew about the ruthless string of international business contacts he had helped set up. He knew about the Mafia-backed black markets for Marlboro cigarettes in the crime-gripped markets of Eastern Europe. He knew he had been ripped off – made the fall guy for

Portillo's global scam after he discovered the Marlboros did not exist. But most terrifyingly of all, he knew he had blown the whistle on the ruthless men behind the deal.

Men who didn't get mad. They got even.

Though he'd never qualified as a chartered accountant, jobbing book-keeper David Wilson made a decent enough living sorting out small tax problems for small Lancashire firms. Of course he was not adverse to the odd 'foreigner' – it paid the bills and maybe allowed him to spoil the daughters he doted on – but he considered himself as straight as the next guy.

The Wilsons moved to Withnell Villa in the mid-1980s from the nearby village of Wheelton, and were well regarded in the local community. Mrs Wilson and their two daughters Lisa and Michelle were all animal lovers and kept a horse, two dogs, poultry and sheep. They had stables at their house and were happy to let local people keep their horses there. The family

Withnell Villa: the Wilson family home and scene of the crime.

bought the house as a derelict shell from the water board at auction for £140,000 because they loved the country life. After moving in they set about renovating the property, pouring almost £100,000 into getting it just right. Set in large, landscaped gardens with panoramic views over the Lancashire countryside, it boasted four bedrooms, two attic bedrooms, four reception rooms, a 1.5 acre paddock and stables.

But locals talked of a 'curse' on Withnell Villa, after a series of unusual deaths at the Victorian property. Two former residents died in the bathroom when they cracked their heads on the bath. One died in a road accident and another had a heart attack. Before the Wilsons moved in, the house had been on the market for a couple of years and no-one from the village had been interested in buying it. As one neighbour chillingly remarked, "No men who have lived there have ever left alive."

Curse or not, the cost of living in the countryside and keeping luxury cars in the garage was proving a burden on the family finances. Then in October 1990, through a mutual business associate, David met a man purporting to be a Mexican colonel by the name of Hector Moretta Portillo who was seeking to set up an anonymous offshore bank account.

In reality, Portillo was the nephew of ex-Mexican President Lopez Portillo, a man who had stolen millions of dollars worth of gold from the Mexican people – a man who, word on the street had it, made President Marcos of the Philippines look like a saint. The man claiming to be Hector Portillo was a swarthy, hefty, moustachioed man of about 5ft 6ins, and in the curious habit of wearing full military dress with a pair of battered old sneakers. He had left the army and was now involved with the United Nations, mixing with high ranking delegates. But more than this, he was involved with shady international commodities, dealing and shifting anything from gold to whisky to sugar to US Treasury bonds and, his personal favourite, Marlboro cigarettes from continent to continent.

Marlboros were second only to the US dollar as dependable recession-proof international currency and fortunes were just waiting to be made. Portillo needed ambitious, greedy middle-men stationed around the world – men with a low profile but a thorough knowledge of finance.

David Wilson fitted the bill perfectly and when the Colonel dangled the bait the Lancastrian swallowed it, hook, line and sinker. Among the mundane book-keeping work he would occasionally be asked to set up offshore tax saving accounts for clients and loved dealing with the exotic locations and mysterious figures who sought them.

❝ when the Colonel dangled the bait the Lancastrian swallowed it... ❞

From the modest surroundings of Leigh Gordon W and Co, his base in a back street terrace of low cost units in Olive Lane, Darwen, Wilson thought he was about to become a real player. Saddled with debts of up to £100,000, in one deal he was about to leave his money worries behind and make his family financially secure forever. All he had to do was find buyers and ship 100 containers of Marlboro cigarettes to Europe – cigarettes put up by Portillo and ready and waiting in Central America. Portillo would then cut him in on the deal and he was made. It was sweet. It was too sweet.

For the lure of easy money and the easy life meant the usually shrewd businessman happily overlooked Portillo's stilted, ham accent; ignored how the deal was becoming increasingly unreal, and ultimately failed to discover the crucial fact that led to his death – that this was not Hector Portillo, but was in fact the alter ego of one Michael Austin, a cheap confidence trickster from the streets of Brooklyn.

Born in 1955, the illegitimate son of Marilyn Austin and an unknown father, he nevertheless enjoyed a fairly well-heeled upbringing. Although he was no Einstein at school and left as soon as he could, young Michael learned his lessons on the mean streets of New York. When it came to hustling, he graduated with honours. He worked behind 50 aliases thanks to a stash of passports stolen from dead people. People like Hector Portillo, whose body was reported by newspapers to have been discovered off the coast of Mexico. Other fake passports were obtained through underworld channels across the world.

Michael Austin, aka Colonel Hector Portillo.

Soon, despite having no visible business, Michael was cruising New York in flash cars and money seemed easy. He recruited a business consultant from a major New York finance house to handle his banking affairs after dangling a £500,000 salary under his nose and telling him his United Nations role forbade him from operating his company accounts himself. But despite an estimated $90m fortune amassed in Swiss bank accounts from his years of crooked wheeler-dealing, the bachelor chose to live with his mother on a modest housing estate in uptown Fort Lee, New Jersey.

Only the ageing blue Rolls Royce in the parking lot outside 1297 Inwood Terrace and his own unnerving policy of silence towards his neighbours gave any hint of his double life.

Friends, usually men, kept quiet but the rumours were flying. He was working for the Mob; he was laundering millions for organised crime. Austin himself even swore he was with the CIA, a claim given credence when he somehow managed to walk away from the authorities after confessing he tried to sell non-existent sugar in the Dominican Republic in 1988. Only once, in 1985, had he put a foot wrong, when he served 18 months for counterfeiting $100 bills.

How much was smokescreen and how much fact may never be fully known, but it is crystal clear that in the closed world of commodities trading and the so-called parallel markets, Austin as Portillo or one of his dozens of other aliases, was a skilled operator.

And the Marlboro scam was possibly his finest to date.

First there was the pitch. By posing as Portillo, the well-connected Mexican, he had access to Marlboro cigarettes made and packed on "ghost shifts" at legitimate Philip Morris factories in the country and labelled "Made in the USA" for added value. Next came the network of clients and a right-hand man in every major country, which in the UK meant David Wilson. Next, bring in insurance experts, add skilled document forgers and financiers happy to turn a blind eye. Then go out there and sell – Austin sold and sold and sold again.

The alleged shipment amounted to 100 containers of Marlboros which in itself amounted to a colossal 48 million packs worth a total of $20m. But Austin was happy to sell the same stuff as many times as he could, always taken on trust, always with some excuse why the cigarettes could not be seen up front.

Fortunately for him, the international banking system helped immeasurably with its so-called "letter of credit" arrangement, which is almost tailor-made for crooks like Austin. Banks in one country talk to banks in another and guarantee payment – providing paperwork is in order – often when goods are still in transit on the high seas. Austin's plan was to get paid from multiple clients all over the world, then scupper the vessel and even claim the insurance. But there was a final stroke of genius.

Austin, masquerading as Portillo, had to distance himself completely from the operation and become untraceable so that in the unlikely event of a problem he could just disappear. Again, through the ever helpful hi-tech US telecommunications system, he simply had to set up a call answering service through a private agency. It was clever, but it may have been too clever. The increasing web of buyers and sellers meant an increasing chance of something going wrong – of someone smelling a rat. And that someone was David Wilson.

As Portillo and Wilson's client list grew and the date of shipping became ever more pressing, it was time to buy a boat. Although he had no experience of shipping or carriage by sea, David set up an offshore business on the Isle of Man called Alamosa Consultants and started looking for a vessel.

By this time ready cash was becoming a problem. In fact bankruptcy was not far from the horizon after the accountant defaulted on loans of £100,000. He was being sued by his own solicitor and was so mired in debt, he asked his daughter Michelle for a £3,000 cheque to help pay off one £20,000 loan. Fortunately one of David's commodities contacts, a Norwegian called Tore Horgen, was more than happy to put up the $1.6m to pay for an ageing old Jamaican cargo ship called the *Gregory* in return for a cut of the cigarette deal.

David cheerfully renamed the 3,400 ton ship the *Lisa Marie* after his youngest daughter, registered it under the Wilson Line banner and sat back, happy in the knowledge that it would soon be docking in Veracruz, Mexico, to pick up a fortune in cigarettes.

The *Lisa Marie*.

In October 1991 he packed off his eldest daughter Michelle to New York's Waldorf Astoria for a face-to-face meeting with the man posing as Portillo. At this point Austin and David exchanged telephone calls almost daily and she had often chatted to 'The Colonel' herself. On arrival in Manhatten his orders were strict, they were to meet in her room alone and her boyfriend, who joined her for the trip, was to wait in the hotel restaurant.

Officially a sum of $10,000 was handed over, which just happened to be the maximum amount of cash legally allowed into the US. The money was for Portillo to pay the *Lisa Marie's* crew of four Finnish officers and ten Honduran deckhands. Throughout the two or three hours Michelle was in Austin's company he maintained his guise, speaking with a Mexican accent.

Three weeks later, on November 12, paperwork arrived showing the *Lisa Marie* had set sail from Miami bound for Hamburg with 50 containers of cigarettes on board. David sat back and waited for the money to start rolling in.
He waited and waited until he finally had to face the awful truth.

Making inquiries, he discovered his ship was not en route, and that it had not even picked up the cargo from Mexico but had managed to haul itself to Venezuela in need of vital repairs. He immediately contacted Norwegian partner Tore Horgen and the two boarded an airplane for South America.

Horgen already had his suspicions about Portillo. Once he had spoken to him on the telephone from Wilson's home and addressed the Mexican colonel in Spanish. His reply did not make sense and he appeared to be struggling with what should have been his native tongue. Horgen handed the phone back to Wilson and warned, "I wouldn't trust that man if I were you David". As they touched down in the Venezuelan capital of Caracas, his fears were soon to be realised. Together they found the rusting old hulk anchored offshore at Puerto Cabello close to the Columbian border.

David Wilson.

Dreading the truth, David ordered the Venezuelan captain to rip open one of the containers strapped to the deck. It was empty – as was the next one and the one after that.

The scale of Austin's rip-off was hammered further home with every empty container. David Wilson's personal wealth together with that of buyers across the world was invested in a $20m cargo which did not exist. He was in big trouble and he knew it. Worse still he harboured suspicions the unravelling cigarette fraud was actually part of an elaborate double cross with Portillo's real cargo intended to be arms and drugs. The fact the *Lisa Marie* was anchored close to the cocaine centre of the world, Columbia, only fuelled this fear.

In a move sure to anger Portillo, his next step was to secure an order barring the vessel from leaving port and so blocking any potential plot to use it to ship drugs into Europe or for it to be scuttled with its phantom cargo of cigarettes for the insurance money. Wilson's buyers lined up for a slice of the Marlboro money included Horgen himself and a host of powerful figures including Russian and Polish army contacts, an underworld gang known as the Polish Mafia, and the Bulgarian Government.

Closer to home David had been working with a Scots-born Texan called James McMillan who had thrown almost $350,000 into the deal. He knew the gun slinging McMillan had a reputation as a tough guy. He owned a collection of 19 firearms, some of which he regularly carried, and despite his cowboy swagger was not a man to double cross. McMillan was once arrested for murder over the shooting of a man who was having an affair with his wife, but never charged. One of his contacts who had been lined up for a slice of the Marlboro shipment, Californian commodities dealer Robert Hochderfter, had offered Wilson a bodyguard for protection after learning of threats made to him by McMillan.

Suddenly David Wilson the international player was once again David Wilson, the husband, father-of-two and Chorley accountant. This was way too big and way too dangerous. It was time to cash his last chip – warn his clients and call the police.

But the police already knew. Some ineptly forged documents had fallen into the hands of the authorities. They smelled a scam and moved quickly.

McMillan had set up a major sales meeting with a group of international dealers at the Rotterdam Hilton. After negotiating with Wilson to buy 56 containers of Marlboro cigarettes, each with a market price of $200,000, he set to work. Delighted the deal was on, McMillan would later recall, "I think we spoke to half of Europe we were so excited." But minutes after making the greatest sales pitch of his life, Dutch River Police stormed the hotel and marched McMillan and five of his associates away at gunpoint. The game, it seemed, was very nearly up.

McMillan, flung into solitary confinement, was furious. Austin, his flawless scam crumbling around him, was furious. And David Wilson, double crossed and hung out to dry, was furious.

McMillan blamed Wilson and dragged him before a Dutch magistrate. Wilson blamed Portillo and blew the whistle on the scam, warning buyers to bale out. He contacted his own 30 investors and shared his fears over the possibility the cigarette scheme was really a front for arms and drug running, advising them to withdraw their credit. Word got back to New York about what the accountant was saying.

Austin, as Portillo, blamed Wilson, and more importantly finally told a colleague, "The gringo limey has to be taken out of the picture, he has to be killed," boasting he would call on members of the Basque terror group ETA to carry out the contract. As fanciful as the claim was, the wheels were put in motion to carry out the deadly threat. At Austin's request a private detective June Helliwell was paid £179 to obtain the address of Wilson's home and the address of his business in Darwen. She picked

" The gringo limey has to be taken out of the picture, he has to be killed. "

the details from a library telephone directory and faxed them to Austin.

A second private detective, Paul Lavey, from Oldham, was dispatched on February 28 to carry out a survey and photograph Wilson's home and office. Believing his clients were seeking help in getting a credit check, Lavey was instructed by a man called Paul Harris to fax the intelligence and precise directions to Austin's office in New York. Paul Harris was sent £1,000 from New York to settle the private detectives' bills and cover his own costs.

By March 4, 1992, Wilson was frantically trying to contact Portillo by telephone, now using a public call box down the road from his home for security. But Austin had vanished, taking his alter ego Hector Portillo with him.

Wilson fought to hide his panic from his family but the cracks were beginning to show. In between desperate attempts to salvage something from the deal, he told Barbara his wife, "That Mexican bastard has set me up but I'm not going to let him drag my name down." He sent the same message on a fateful fax to Portillo and signed off by saying he was coming to get him.

Wilson had already spoken to Scotland Yard detectives a couple of weeks earlier as part of the Dutch investigation and used the opportunity to confess all about the Marlboro scam, pinning all of the blame on Austin. He told officers he genuinely believed the cigarettes had existed right up until he stepped on board the *Lisa Marie* in Venezuela.

But Austin was way ahead of the game. He had already hired the private detectives to case the Wilson house and even as David plotted his revenge the two assassins, with firearms loaded and ready, were on their way to Chorley.

March 5, 1992, and everything David Wilson had ever really cared for; his wife, his children, his home, were at the mercy of two faceless men with loaded guns. Lisa, 24, was still hysterical, and Barbara was in tears. Michelle tried to comfort them.

"Everyone on the floor!" ordered one of the men in a menacing half French-half Irish accent, "just do as you're told and no harm will come to you. We've just come to talk to David."

Lisa's fiancé Mark was first. His hands and feet were bound tightly with blue vinyl tape. Then David. That was the men out of the way. The smaller gunman then levelled his gun at Lisa and commanded her to rip down the curtain cords. He pulled out a knife and slashed at the thick cord before ordering the women into the lounge and tying them up. Then, in true Hollywood gangster style, he turned the television up to full volume. With an odd twist of conscience the gunman then offered Barbara a cushion to make her more comfortable.

Back in the kitchen the wiry hitman turned to David who was still on the floor and still petrified. "You know why we're here, don't you David?" he started. David shook his head, "No."

"Of course you do. It's over the money you took." David shook his head again and pleaded, "What money? I haven't taken any money." But the gunman was unmoved, "Come on David," he said, "you know you've taken the money... and somebody has paid me a lot of money to come here and talk to you about it."

David continued to plead his innocence. But he knew he was really pleading for his life. Still calm, his voice unwavering, the gunman had heard enough, and ordered David Wilson to get up and walk out to the adjoining double garage. The family heard two dull thuds from somewhere in the night. And David Wilson was dead.

> **❝ The family heard two dull thuds from somewhere in the night. ❞**

In the house, Lisa had managed to work her slender wrists free and immediately ran to the kitchen to free Mark. Within minutes the rest of the family was released. They checked the telephones. The lines were ripped out.

Unwilling or unable to equate the two dull cracks they had heard with gunshots, they were convinced David had been kidnapped. Jumping in the family Mercedes they drove frantically to a village phone box and dialled 999. It was not until they returned some minutes later that the powerful headlights on their car picked out the full horror.

In the shadows of the garage David Wilson's body lay slumped face down on the floor with his hands tied behind his back. He had been forced to kneel on the cold concrete floor and shot twice in the back of the head.

By the early hours of March 6, two things had happened. Austin had begun to realise exactly what he'd done, and Lancashire police had mobilised hundreds of officers in a massive operation to hunt down the killers. Austin had broken the cardinal rule of conmen – never let it get personal. He'd had his cash and a good run for his money and normally he would have just killed off his Colonel Portillo character and disappeared into the ether to plan his next scam. No guns and no regrets. David Wilson could have identified him, but it was more than that – the small time accountant had had the gall to challenge Austin's authority.

Within hours of the shooting, Austin's mobile phone was taking calls from across the world from contacts staggered and frightened by the assassination which was prime time news on TV stations across the globe. He remained stony-faced but he was getting nervous. He barked into the receiver as call after call pointed the finger, "It's nothing to do with me. Wilson was involved with the wrong people. It's South Africa, it's the Mafia! You want to ask James McMillan who done it!"

As the calls mounted up, Austin really started to lose it: "He shoulda kept away from them people in the Far East. He was smuggling heroin! That's what happens when you double cross people!" Another suspicious caller warned Austin to get some good legal people. He replied, "I got the best lawyers in the world, name of Smith & Wesson," before slamming down the telephone.

Meanwhile, an incident room was set up in Lancashire under Detective Superintendent Bob Denmark. Thousands of man-hours of painstaking paperwork were married with officers travelling to the four corners of the globe to establish a link between Wilson and Austin. New links were also forged between Lancashire Police, the FBI, US Customs and the outspoken Mob-smashing New York assistant district attorney Charles Rose.

Only days after the murder, Bob Denmark was convinced they had identified their man.

Charles Rose was contacted to get a warrant and confront Austin who was heading for the airport. They missed him but, undaunted, US Customs agents Diane Hansen and Jody Foresta, who were based at the towering World Trade Center in

New York City, stayed on his tail. They combined hi-tech electronic surveillance techniques with plain, old fashioned stake outs and on July 15 they pounced on Austin as he made his way to the giant Trump Tower block in Manhattan. He was about to splash out $2.3m for an apartment in the prestigious 5th Avenue development. Adopting the guise of Michael Bond he was sealing the deal through a company called Universal Exports, the fictional cover name for the British secret service in the *James Bond* films.

He went quietly. No guns, no fight. He even weakly complained that the handcuffs were hurting his wrists. It was day one of a 1,000-day legal fight which ended with the phantom known as Hector Portillo in the dock at Carlisle Crown Court amid scenes of unprecedented security. Throughout the two-month trial, police snipers, armed with semi-automatic weapons, were stationed on the roof of the court. Each day Austin was whisked to court by a heavy escort, with dozens of armed police officers and motorbike outriders alongside. A procession of colourful characters from the secret lives of David Wilson and Michael Austin took to the stand in the Cumbrian border city to shine a light on the murky twilight world of commodities dealing.

The Norwegian businessman Tore Horgen, the Scottish-Texan dealer James McMillan, Austin's allies in New York and London, brokers from across Europe and America, private detectives. After hearing their stories, the jury of seven women and five men took just two hours to return a guilty verdict, condemning Austin to life behind bars with the words of Judge Mr Justice Kay ringing in his ears:

"It is clear from the evidence that David Wilson had no concept of what he was getting involved in and that those he was dealing with would lose very substantial amounts of money. When he found out, he did not leave the victims to their own fate but set about repairing the damage as best he could."

"You tried to frighten him off with threats, but you could not, so you arranged to have him killed. His killing was a savage and awful act and you are guilty of the most serious form of wicked and evil behaviour."

> **"** ...you are guilty of the most serious form of wicked and evil behaviour. **"**

But what was to be the most complex and lengthy case ever undertaken by Lancashire CID was far from over. While Austin tried every legal trick in the book to resist deportation from America to face trial, taking his case right up to the US Supreme Court, back in the UK detectives based in Lancashire had been busy. Austin's middleman in England was first to be locked up for life for his part in the execution.

Stephen Schepke boasted of living in a James Bond world of international arms dealing, of Mig jet fighters, cut price Russian helicopters, gold trading, Israeli guns and the SAS. But the facade was as thin as the glossy weapons brochures he sent out from his terraced house in Sidcup, Kent. In fact, his life was closer to that of Hollywood daydreamer Walter Mitty.

Fixer Stephen Schepke arranged Wilson's murder.

Schepke claimed he dealt in intelligence and supplied guns to the SAS and even the ultra secret British 14 Intelligence Unit operating in Northern Ireland. And like his New York sidekick, he too operated under an alias – Paul Harris. The same Paul Harris who tasked the private detectives to pull together details on Wilson's country home at Austin's request. But more often than moving through the global underworld, the self-confessed alcoholic was to be found downing a drink, or one of his favoured "liquid lunches," in the local Conservative Club.

Heavily in debt, Schepke was given to rambling incoherently and his home and personal life could politely be described as chaotic. The 46-year-old, married to Barbara, was born in Oldham. He moved to Doncaster at the age of five, then

Blackpool and at the age of 18 left to travel abroad, finally getting a job in Canada. It was not long before he returned to the UK and gained O and A levels before setting off on his travels again, this time studying art in Zurich and specialising in fine art restoration in Nuremburg. He returned to the UK again and took up a job at the *Kentish Mercury* newspaper, but restless as ever, he was soon on the move again after falling out with his editor, and this time he set himself up in art and arms restoration.

Despite his drink problem he was granted a firearms dealer's licence and, with a bank overdraft, attempted to break into the international arms market from a workshop over his house. Schepke & Sons began with modest aspirations, mainly repairing weapons. But his ideas grew from the ambitious – printing glossy brochures for distribution all over the world – to the incredible, discussing plans for a shipment of arms for a coup d'état in Central America. He even told police he could get four Mig 29 fighter planes and 20 Russian helicopters on the cheap. But Schepke was operating way out of his depth. He was contacted by Austin who retained him as his right-hand man in the UK, and the pair arranged to meet at Charing Cross Station in London. The New Yorker wanted information and manpower.

At the meeting he told Schepke how Wilson had blown the whistle on him and, fixing him with a cold stare, asked "Do you know anyone who could blow the hell out of Wilson?"

Schepke hired the two private detectives to spy on David Wilson and set up Swiss bank accounts to pay them. He also provided the hit men. Veteran Stephen Playle worked as a chef at the Black Horse pub in Sidcup. He had been a private in the Parachute Regiment for just under three years and served in Oman, Canada and the Falklands Islands. His lifelong friend and fellow ex-servicemen, Michael Crossley, was a regular at the pub.

Hitman Michael Crossley was found guilty of the murder of Lancashire accountant David Wilson and the unlawful imprisonment of his daughter Michelle, by a jury at Liverpool Crown Court.

It was at the pub that fellow regular Schepke enlisted the pair to carry out the hit on Wilson and provided the weapons.

Crossley and Schepke travelled from Kent to Lancashire in the days before the execution to finalise their deadly plot. Then, on the day of the murder, Crossley borrowed his wife Alison's red Vauxhall Chevette and headed north with Playle. Detectives arrested the linkman four days after the execution after receiving information from the private detectives. They found details of the killers' telephone numbers in his address book and on scraps of paper in his wallet. They also recovered scribbled notes in his possession about Austin and Wilson, along with several letters about Marlboro cigarettes.

Crucially for detectives, Playle had made one error in the meticulously planned execution of David Wilson. A solitary thumbprint was discovered on the blue tape used to bind the accountant's hands. With Playle's thumbprint, sightings of Crossley's car and the details of the pair's telephone numbers found on the man who hired them for murder, their number was up.

Hitman Stephen Playle, 34, who was found guilty of David Wilson's murder.

But unbeknown to the murder squad, Schepke had already been involved in his own treacherous game of double cross. In the weeks before the murder he was also feeding information to the Metropolitan Police and Lloyds shipping investigators. He told them of the cigarette fraud, the fake documents and plans to sabotage the ship. Schepke planned to win both ways; he had been promised a cut of the pay-off if the cigarette con was successful, but if it wasn't, he hoped to pocket a fat reward from Lloyds. With David Wilson's murder, Schepke's game was up and in the end he realised the deadly company he was keeping and took to sleeping with a loaded Browning pistol under his pillow.

The conspiracy had been cracked, from the American criminal mastermind who ordered the execution in a quiet Lancashire village through his British Mr Fix-It, to the men who pulled the trigger on an ordinary businessman who spotted the main chance.

And died for it.

CHAPTER TEN

In the shadow of the bombers

Janet Murgatroyd, Preston, June 16, 1996

CALMLY, the driver steered the burgundy Ford Granada into a residents' parking bay a couple of hundred yards from Preston railway station. After parking the car, three men jumped out and walked the short distance from Mount Street, past Bethany Convent to the station and faded into the crowd of weekend travellers.

Shortly after 11.15am on June 15, 1996, the largest bomb detonated on the UK mainland since the Second World War ripped the heart out of Manchester city centre. Police had managed to clear the immediate area before the blast tore into Corporation Street between the Arndale Centre and Marks and Spencer store. But the sheer scale of the explosion sent shards of glass from surrounding shop windows hurtling hundreds of yards along the main shopping streets, injuring 200 people.

When Janet Murgatroyd heard news of the atrocity she scrapped plans to catch the train into Manchester. Instead she called into St Wilfrid's Church, in Preston, and lit a candle. Janet had planned to meet up with her friend Fiona Watson and hop on the train and take the 50-minute journey to Manchester. The pals were excited about a dream trip travelling around Europe they were preparing for later in the summer. They hoped to fly out to the Greek island of Rhodes and spend ten weeks backpacking around the continent before heading back in time for Janet to resume her studies at the University of Central Lancashire in September. The highlight of the trip was to be Janet's 21st birthday in September, when the friends aimed to celebrate the big day in Italy.

The explosion forced them to change their plan, and they decided instead to head into Preston to look for clothes for their holiday. It was a sunny day and the pubs were packed as the city was in a party mood while the girls wandered from shop to shop eyeing up new outfits. The nation was gripped by football fever with the Euro '96 tournament in full swing and Preston was no different. Every vantage point in every shop, home and car was flying the flag of St George as millions of people were swept along with the sporting pageant being staged on English soil for the first time.

On that Saturday afternoon, the home side beat the auld enemy Scotland at Wembley with the nation's poster boy Paul Gascoigne assuming the starring role with a breathtaking goal late in the game securing a 2-0 victory. In the warm sunshine, thousands of revellers were ready to party into the night and Janet telephoned home to tell her mum she would be staying out to join in the fun. Dressed casually in jeans and a white short sleeved top the 20-year-old was not kitted out for the city's more fashionable bars, so after spending some time at the Wall Street bar they headed for the popular student pubs along Friargate.

Janet Murgatroyd was the only child of the marriage between David and Mary Murgatroyd. Her parents separated when she was young and Janet was brought up in Broad Oak Green, Penwortham, by her mum, with whom she had an especially close relationship. She was also the apple of her dad's eye and remained in contact with him despite the marital split although, with one thing and another, the pair had not seen each other since February.

Growing up she was a happy, spirited child who played for endless hours with other children on the local green. She went to St Teresa's Catholic Primary School in Penwortham, and was the larger than life character in her class. Years after she left, teachers would remember the year as 'Janet Murgatroyd's class' such was her vibrant, bubbly character.

Intelligent and hardworking, Janet was a popular pupil at All Hallows Catholic High School where she was keen on sport and captained the school hockey team. She went on to study at Cardinal Newman College in Preston where she was well liked by her peers and achieved excellent grades. Her popularity saw her elected as a student representative, giving her a role liaising with college staff on behalf of classmates.

Janet also kept up her passion for sport and was a key member of the Cardinal Newman netball team, ranked at the time as one of the finest in the county. For extra spending money she worked at the French Bistro in Preston so she could go out partying with pals. After leaving college Janet enrolled at the University of Central Lancashire to study for a law degree. To help pay her way, she secured a part-time job in the Crime Input Bureau at Lancashire Police headquarters in Hutton.

Despite her choice of course, Janet had told colleagues that she dreamed of a job in the music industry after graduation. An energetic and confident person, she was very driven in striving for her goals in life and had successfully passed all of the elements of her first year course at UCLan.

But everything was not happy in Janet's world.

Despite her outward confidence she had endured an abusive relationship with a former boyfriend. On one occasion the thug she called 'The Pitbull' waited for Janet outside Preston's Legends nightclub and when she emerged, he pounced. She was dragged by her hair, pulled through bushes, punched to the floor and kicked. Each time she got up he knocked her down again. In a common response from victims of domestic violence she blamed herself for the abuse and convinced herself she had deserved it. The brute was known to police and had made death threats towards Janet when the pair split up.

Now single, Janet was enjoying the Euro '96 carnival mood in popular students' haunt The Adelphi when she got chatting to fellow student Brendan Connell.

Janet and Fiona had become split up, and Fiona would later recall, "We couldn't have been happier. We were both on top of the world that day, we thought nothing was going to stop us from here on in. We had been in the pub quite a lot of the afternoon and it was going to be our last night out before we went on our holidays so we were making it a good night."

Janet and Brendan enjoyed a few drinks and decided to head to the other end of Friargate to the Old Black Bull. In the car park outside the back of the pub they kissed and fondled for five to ten minutes, but after more than six hours drinking Janet was, by now, very drunk. At one

Janet Murgatroyd had her whole life ahead of her.

point she stumbled in a loading bay at the back of the pub but seemed unhurt and declined Brendan's offer to take her to hospital. Realising just how intoxicated Janet was, the accounting student believed it would be wrong to take advantage of her and encouraged her to head home. He walked her along Fishergate and Church Street when he spotted a group of his friends. Before saying his goodbyes to Janet he took her to the cab rank close to Yates' pub and urged her to get a taxi home. She did not take his advice.

Instead Janet made the fatal decision to walk the couple of miles through town back home. It was 12.30am. Within an hour she would lie dying on the banks of the River Ribble, the victim of a sustained and savage beating.

CCTV footage taken from the Fishergate shopping centre would reveal it took Janet 20 minutes to stagger the first few hundred yards. Witnesses would later describe the blonde weaving along the thoroughfare, past Preston railway station, wending her way towards Penwortham. At one point she was seen slumped on the ground close to the station but refused assistance from a concerned passer-by. A second man who came across Janet's stricken figure collapsed on the pavement showed less concern.

Drug addict Raymond Hayes was walking home when he spotted her purse a foot away and an opportunity for easy pickings to feed his £50-a-day heroin habit. The barman rifled her bag and stole a silver chain and locket and her cash before leaving Janet collapsed on the floor. If she had wanted to walk the few yards to the station taxi rank and get a cab home, she could no longer afford it. As she stumbled on towards home she saw a man she recognised but declined an offer to walk with him and a friend down Broadgate, saying she was heading for the new river bridge.

It was 1.10am by the time she reached the corner of Broadgate with Penwortham Bridge. Motorist John Livesey spotted Janet lurching across the bridge. The young student was waving her arms in the air as if attempting to hail a taxi. Concerned at her state, the late hour and the fact she was alone, Mr Livesey's mother urged him to stop and pick her up but he refused because he thought she might be sick in his car. When he looked in his rear view mirror, he saw Janet step into the road and turn around as if making her way back towards Preston. A few minutes later cab driver Ashleigh Sperren saw a man chasing after a woman down the middle of the road across the bridge. The woman appeared to have been running as well. It was to be the last time the pretty, young student would be seen alive. She was just a mile and a half from home.

At 1.30am two brothers crossing the bridge heard a muffled, high-pitched wail in bushes at Priory Park close to the southern banks of the Ribble. Jonathan and Paul Richardson turned to see where the noise was coming from and heard the sound of snapping twigs being trampled in the undergrowth. They saw the shadowy figure of a man crouching down about 15 metres away, but were unable to get a good look at him because of the darkness.

At lunchtime on Sunday, June 16, a dog walker ambling along the banks of the River Ribble spotted what he thought was a body floating face down in the water with long blonde hair. He shouted to a speedboat driver pulling a water skier along the Ribble for help. A man in his garden nearby was alerted to the unfolding drama and rang the police.

The boat pulled over to the shore close to The Continental pub and dragged Janet's body on board. She had been stripped naked and brutally attacked. Her body was covered in scratches caused by being dragged through the dense riverside undergrowth by her killer.

A post mortem examination showed she had been beaten about the head, knocked unconscious and stamped on before being dumped in the river. She suffered 59 separate injuries, mainly to the head and face, including a fractured jaw. Although unconscious and suffering from injuries that would have proved fatal, Janet was alive when she entered the water and remained so for at least four hours.

“ She suffered 59 separate injuries... ”

Investigators believe she was probably lying on a sand bank below the high water mark then when the tidal flow came in, she was washed into the river by the incoming tide. Unconscious and unable to move, Janet drowned. Police suspected she had also been the victim of a sexual assault. Janet's mother Mary was given the grim task of identifying her daughter's body.

Lancashire Police drafted in one of the force's most senior murder squad officers to head the investigation into the killing. Detective Superintendent Graham Gooch put together a 50-strong team based in an incident room not far from where Janet worked at Hutton headquarters. It was a photograph taken of Janet for her police security pass which was blown up on a poster and circulated around Preston. With her curly blonde hair and chirpy smile, it was to become an enduring image.

A £5,000 reward was put up by the Crimestoppers Trust for any information leading to the arrest and conviction of the killer. The sum was later matched by the *Lancashire Evening Post.*

Police at the murder scene on the bank of the River Ribble.

Mountain rescue experts were called in to help police officers conduct a painstaking, fingertip search of land near the Ribble. Bushes at the spot where Janet was dragged down the riverbank were cut off at the base, tagged and labelled and sent for forensic examination. Blood found spattered on one was analysed and found to be the student's. It was one of the few pieces of forensic evidence gathered from the scene and was later destroyed when a forensic laboratory was petrol bombed in an unrelated attack.

Janet's clothing and jewellery were recovered from the area close to where the Richardson brothers had heard a disturbance a few hours earlier. Only her stone-washed Wrangler jeans were missing despite a call from a group of children who claimed to have found them while playing in bushes near to the murder scene. When officers returned to the riverbank they had vanished.

Police launched a massive search of the River Ribble for the jeans. A police rescue team from St Annes and the force's helicopter coordinated the search at the Broadgate end of the river. Rescuers recovered clothing and rubbish but nothing connected to the death.

Detectives decided to employ the help of the latest scientific research used in industry to help pinpoint where Janet's body had entered the river. Experts from nuclear giant BNFL produced a computer model of the Ribble Estuary. Studying tide times and the moment they suspected Janet was attacked, they worked out where her body must have been dumped in the water for it to have been washed up by The Continental.

Computer profiling was used to probe possible links with 200 other unsolved murders across the United Kingdom stretching back 20 years, while experts drew up a profile of the likely killer.

This study was released by Acting Det Supt Colin Maloney who said, "This man carried out a blitz attack on a very vulnerable victim. The offender had a great rage or anger which was demonstrated by the attack.

"He was disorganised and showed a lack of planning as the attack was so close to the main road. This indicates he is at the younger end of the spectrum. It is likely he has a history of violence against women which might have been manifested in previous convictions, although not necessarily.

LANCASHIRE CONSTABULARY

MURDER

JANET MURGATROYD was murdered at the side of the Penwortham road bridge between 1am - 2am on Sunday, 16th June, 1996.

WERE YOU IN THE AREA?
CAN YOU HELP?

Ring 01772 614444 or contact any police officer

Call CRIMESTOPPERS on 0800 555 111

"Looking at other murders it is almost certain that this offender has knowledge of the area. He will be familiar with or have previous knowledge of the murder scene and it is likely he lives, or did live, in the area."

In the weeks after the killing, police released images of Janet caught on security cameras from businesses around Preston town centre in the hours before her death. More than 1,400 statements were taken as the incident room phones buzzed with people offering information. Officers travelled the length and breadth of the country from Winchester to Carlisle and from Hull to Chester investigating possible suspects. A reconstruction of Janet's last known movements was put together with a fellow student playing the role of the murdered student.

Det Insp Graham Bamber told the *Lancashire Evening Post*, "This man showed absolutely no mercy. The fierceness of the attack was such that Janet could never have survived. Janet only did one thing wrong. She believed the care and protection the community had afforded her for the 20 years of her life would always be there. Unfortunately on this night her view was very tragically let down."

Police reconstruction of Janet crossing Penwortham Bridge close to where she was killed.

On June 28, hundreds of friends and family packed into St Teresa's Church, Penwortham, for a memorial service. Just four days later an inquest hearing was told how Janet was beaten and left for dead by the Ribble until the tide carried her body away.

The official cause of death was recorded as drowning.

On September 3, 1996, Janet was buried at Hill Road Cemetery in a private ceremony after a funeral service attended by hundreds of mourners at St Teresa's RC Church. The service was so packed, some people were forced to sit on the street outside to listen. It was 11 weeks after Janet was found dead and five days before what would have been her 21st birthday.

The same day the BBC's *Crimewatch* programme broadcast a nationwide appeal. An actress played Janet in a ten-minute reconstruction of her last day, and the programme featured heart-rending interviews with best friend Fiona Watson and Janet's mum Mary, who made an emotional appeal for witnesses. The broadcast attracted more than 50 calls to the incident room. But none provided the breakthrough police were looking

BBC *Crimewatch* reconstruction of Janet's last movements.

for in the hunt for the killer who had taken the life of their popular young colleague.

It would be three years with the police investigation scaled right down before a dramatic and unexpected twist in the inquiry.

Taxi driver Valie Ugradar was driving through Penwortham in the early hours of August 2, 1999, when he was flagged down by a man at the side of the road. He pulled his cab to the kerbside and his passenger jumped in and asked to be taken to a police station. As Mr Ugradar drove away, the man started sobbing and the driver asked him if everything was alright. The passenger replied he had, "done something bad". In a clearly distressed state he added he would be "going away for a long time" when police learned of the crime he had committed. Mr Ugradar asked him what he had done and the man replied, "Never mind, you will hear it in the news tomorrow."

Disturbed at what he was hearing, the taxi driver headed for Penwortham police station as it was nearer than Preston. As he drove along Cop Lane he spotted two police officers investigating a burglar alarm ringing out at the primary school. He waved at the officers, stopped and his passenger got out. As he approached PC Denis Halliwell, he told the officer his name, age and address. PC Halliwell then asked him what he had done and the man replied, "murder". More than three years after Janet Murgatroyd's battered body was found floating in the Ribble, police finally had what seemed to be the major breakthrough they had been searching for.

Andrew Greenwood was a loner with few friends. Bespectacled and slightly built, he cut an inoffensive figure. But beneath the shy exterior he had grown obsessed with the murder of the pretty, blonde student one mile from his home. At the time of the murder, Greenwood lived alone in a dark and dingy flat at The Maltings, in Penwortham. By a bizarre coincidence, the development was also home to thief Raymond Hayes, one of the last people to see Janet alive as he robbed her as she lay drunk on the pavement close to Preston railway station. It is unlikely the pair knew each other as Greenwood was not known to mingle with fellow tenants.

" Andrew Greenwood was a loner with few friends. "

He rarely spoke to any stranger unless he had been drinking. His next door neighbour never spoke to him once in four years. A caretaker at the development described him as the perfect tenant, never offering up any trouble. He divided his time between his flat and a relative's home in Lostock Hall.

One of three children, Greenwood's parents Philip and Joyce, split up when he was a teenager. He went to Brownedge St Mary's High School, in Bamber Bridge, where he gained eight GCSEs. But despite his exam success, Greenwood never had any faith in his own abilities and suffered from low self-esteem. He went on to get a series of clerical jobs but never stuck with any for long. Greenwood had suffered from depression from the age of 18 and masked his illness with alcohol.

Andrew Greenwood.

During the summer of 1996 he had been unemployed for 12 months and was doing a part-time statistics course at Preston College. But in the weeks before his roadside confession to Janet's murder, his mental health was on the slide. Without warning he walked out of his job at Zebra Technologies in Fulwood, Preston, and about three weeks later, on a Wednesday, slashed his wrist. The cuts, to his left wrist, were superficial. The following Sunday, Greenwood confessed to PC Halliwell. After admitting to murder he was cautioned.

PC Halliwell asked who he had murdered and Greenwood said, "Janet Murgatroyd, three years ago." Asked how he had murdered the student he replied, "I punched and kicked her and left her on the riverbank. I saw her on the bridge. I talked to her and she laughed at me. It's been preying on my mind for three years – it was the day of the football match versus Scotland."

Greenwood was taken to Leyland police station and the following day began a series of five interviews led by Det Chief Insp Ian Kennedy. Over a total of three and a half hours he made a series of detailed, taped confessions to murder squad officers.

In the hours before Janet's murder Greenwood told the murder team he had been out watching the football with his friends in Preston, drinking about six pints in the afternoon and a further two pints before going to his father's home for tea. He went out again about 6.30pm and met a friend before resuming drinking heavily at the Sumpter Horse pub in Penwortham. Greenwood said he had been feeling bad on the night and was paranoid because his contact lenses were irritating him.

He believed the friends he was playing pool with were laughing at him. He stormed off after telling one of the group, "I feel like killing myself or I am going to kill someone."

As he walked the streets in a drunken haze, Greenwood explained, he was feeling depressed for a combination of reasons. He was lonely and wanted someone to talk to. Heading towards Preston town centre Greenwood claimed he saw Janet near the Bridge Inn by the river – an area some way from what should have been her journey home. He did not know her but she was obviously drunk. Greenwood outlined to police how he tried speaking to her and offered to walk her home or get her a taxi, but she refused and laughed off his attempts at conversation. He kept on talking but she became edgy and began running back the way she had come.

In his confession, he said, "She was drunk, I thought I would chat her up. I tried to kiss her but she kept backing away. I thought she would be easy because she was drunk. I started chasing her to calm her down. She was getting hysterical and if anyone saw me it looked really bad. I was thinking 'I'm going to get done.' She was screaming 'Leave me alone.' She was getting very panicky. I thought 'I'm not going to hurt her. I'm just going to talk to her.'"

When Greenwood caught up with Janet he grabbed her and put his hand over her mouth to calm her down. He confessed, "I thought, I'm making the situation worse. What can I do, I cannot leave it like this?"

Greenwood said he dragged the drunken 20-year-old into bushes, punching her up to five times. When she fell to the floor, he claimed, he kicked her repeatedly in the head. He admitted to detectives he had "totally lost it".

As she lay unconscious he described removing her clothes in an attempt to avoid detection. "I realised what I had done and took her clothes off," he said, fearing his blood might have been on her clothes. He then hurled the body into the river with such force in his drunken state he almost fell in himself. He said, "I was panicking, it was like a rush. I stood there and saw her body float downstream. It got caught up on the bank and then continued."

Greenwood said he later learnt she was not dead when he threw her into the water. "I should have stopped and got help," he said. Greenwood described then how he made his way to his home at The Maltings through Penwortham Holme Allotments, which lay behind the riverbank. He got in at about 3.30am and told investigators he felt like killing himself. The next morning he thought he had simply had a bad dream but everything came back when he read the *Lancashire Evening Post* report about Janet's death.

In the days and weeks ahead, when friends spoke about the killing he revealed he would always "try to change the subject." After the reconstruction on *Crimewatch* he felt "half relieved that they had not got anything on me, and half feeling that I should give myself up." Over the intervening years articles in papers, such as on the anniversary of the death, brought it all back to him, he added.

CCTV footage of the murder victim.

Alongside the confession Greenwood sketched a diagram, detailing Janet's injuries. He wound up his confession by telling officers, "I wish to say sorry for my actions. It is not like me. I will carry on repenting like I have done over the past three years."

On August 3, 1999, Andrew Philip Greenwood appeared before Chorley Magistrates Court and was charged with the murder of Janet Murgatroyd. Despite the detailed nature of the 25-year-old's confession, nagging doubts remained. Did a man with no history of violent behaviour really batter the young student and leave her to drown in the hours before dawn on a summer's day?

Extensive forensic tests could find no link between Greenwood and either the crime scene or Janet's body. None of the witnesses who saw her walking home alone reported spotting anyone who fitted his description. Could the mentally disturbed young man have made a false confession after becoming obsessed with the highest profile murder in Preston for many years?

On December 16, 1999, the case against Greenwood was sensationally dropped. He had already withdrawn his confession. The Crown Prosecution Service ruled there was not enough evidence to go to trial at the crown court. The CPS said there was insufficient evidence to get a conviction and questioned discrepancies in Greenwood's statements. A CPS spokesman explained, "It is the role of the CPS to review independently evidence supplied by the police. The case has been exhaustively reviewed by senior CPS lawyers and regularly discussed with the police.

"Statements made by Mr Greenwood to the police have been carefully scrutinised against other evidence in the case, and significant inconsistencies emerged. There is no forensic evidence to link Mr Greenwood with the crime. After thorough consideration, the CPS has decided there is insufficient evidence to provide a realistic prospect of conviction.

"We are as anxious as the police to see progress made in this horrific case, but the CPS cannot proceed unless the evidential test is passed. We are always willing to look again at cases in the light of any new evidence."

The verdict angered Lancashire Police.

A terse statement issued by the constabulary said, "Following lengthy consideration of the evidence, the CPS accepts that there is a prima facie case, and more than a bare prima facie case, against Greenwood, but it does not meet CPS guidelines." The man at the head of the murder investigation, Det Supt Graham Gooch went one step further saying, "We are very disappointed by the decision of the Crown Prosecution Service. Our view is that this is eminently a question for a jury and should have been left to a jury to make a decision. We are also surprised that the CPS made their decision without the benefit of advice from leading counsel."

Greenwood had spent three months in Preston Prison before being released to a bail hostel in Carlisle just days before his shock release. His solicitor, John O'Donnell, said his client "emphatically" denied any involvement with the murder of Janet before adding, "There is not a shred of independent evidence against him. In spite of an investigation lasting three years, the police have failed to solve this crime." And he called for the police to "re-examine their efforts to do this".

Lancashire Police did not need reminding, with Det Chief Insp Ian Kennedy vowing, "The investigation is still open and will not be closed until Janet's killer is convicted."

The murder squad went back to work and for the next nine months re-examined their evidence. An international expert in the field of false confessions was drafted in to look again at Greenwood's statements. Professor Gisli Gudjonnson, a clinical psychologist, professor of forensic psychology and head of forensic psychology services at Kings College, London, had dealt with some of the world's biggest miscarriage of justice cases during a 20-year career; including those against Derek Bentley, who was hanged in 1953 for a murder he did not commit; the Guildford four, who were wrongly convicted of IRA bomb attacks in England in 1974; and the Birmingham six, who were wrongly jailed for killing 21 people in the pub bombings of 1975. His studies would bolster the new evidence which once again pointed the finger at Andrew Greenwood.

On October 2, 2000, a summons was issued ordering him to appear before Chorley Magistrates to again face charges of murder. Prosecutor Peter Wright QC said the CPS had "significant" new information which "shed a wholly different light" on the proceedings and on Greenwood's initial confession to police. He said that the defendant's own psychological make-up was "central to the case" and a new report proved this initial confession to police was likely to be based on fact. This report proved Greenwood's initial confession corroborated with the actual injuries suffered by Janet – facts which only the murderer could have known.

Mr Wright said Greenwood talked of blows being rained down in a perpendicular fashion on Janet and attempts to muffle her screaming, both facts borne out by forensic evidence. He said, "This is not the type of detail that can be alighted upon at random." Once again Greenwood's legal team went on the attack, accusing the police of making a "maverick" decision in continuing their pursuit of their client.

But this time Greenwood would stand trial. The four-week hearing began at Liverpool Crown Court on October 2, 2002. The jury was told it was the Crown's case that Greenwood's interview was "too detailed, too elaborate to be a charade."

During the confession, replayed to the court, Greenwood said if it was anyone else, he would "throw the key away." As he finished his account of the night Janet died, Greenwood added that he felt he "could not cope" with 20 years in jail and would rather not be alive. During the interview Greenwood was told by Det Chief Insp Ian Kennedy, "It is important that we talk about things on the night that you can remember and not what you saw on *Crimewatch* or read in the papers." But that was exactly the argument put forward by Greenwood.

His lawyers told the court he had become obsessed with Janet's murder and, in his unstable mental state, had convinced himself he was the killer. On the Tuesday after the killing, Greenwood explained to the jury, he passed a *Lancashire Evening Post* billboard which featured the murder inquiry. "I read the article and was fascinated by it because it was local," he said. He carried on buying the newspaper in the following weeks and followed the investigation closely. "It grabbed my attention – being local it added to the fascination."

He had troubles with his job and "wanted to put my own worries into perspective" by concentrating on the murder case. As the publicity continued he said he wanted to find out more about the murder and when drinking he began to believe he had been speaking to Janet on the night of the murder: "When I was sober it seemed ridiculous," he told jurors. Eventually his fascination with the murder, in his own words, "began to turn against me."

"By about one or two months after the murder I had convinced myself I was the killer," he said. "I wanted to be punished. The more it went on with no-one being arrested, the more I believed I was guilty," he said. Greenwood began to "punish himself" for problems in his life by believing he was the man who police wanted for the killing and the *Crimewatch* TV programme reinforced this feeling.

Greenwood said he had used the details obtained from press and television coverage in his confession. He insisted that he first started thinking that he had not killed Janet while on remand in prison. But prosecutors revealed Greenwood had correctly described the appearance of a passerby who nearly disturbed the killer, despite the reconstruction showing him with a different hairstyle. He also recalled Janet had been wearing a gold chain – a fact never reported by the media.

Prosecutor Paul Reid told the courtroom, "He displayed a great deal of knowledge about the murder, much more extensive than you would expect from someone who may have happened to read reports in the local newspapers or viewed *Crimewatch* some three years previously."

When his home was searched, the police found no press cuttings or video of the *Crimewatch* programme. "If, as the defendant now claims, he based his confession to the police on what he read and remembered from newspapers and what he had seen on *Crimewatch*, you may think that he had a remarkable memory for detail published a very long time before he made that confession."

His legal team argued that there was not a shred of forensic or DNA evidence to implicate him either at the murder scene, on his clothes or on the body. Greenwood had woken up the morning after the murder in the same clothes he had been wearing the night before. There was no sign on his T-shirt or jeans that had been involved in a frenzied attack on an overgrown riverbank, and he had no scratches. Greenwood told the jury that he remembered saying goodbye to his friend after an evening out together drinking on the night of the murder, and the next thing he remembered was waking up in his flat the next morning.

But a series of letters Greenwood wrote to his family from Preston Prison shortly after his arrest in August 1999 were presented to the court. In one letter he wrote, "Everything is starting to get blurry. I cannot get the story straight at the moment, maybe it's the medication. I probably have done it in a blackout." Greenwood wrote that he had been asked by another prisoner why he had given himself in three years after Janet's death in 1996. "I would not be human if I lied for my actions for the rest of my life," he wrote. In a third letter he wrote, "I feel worse knowing I killed two people because the guy who found her in the river committed suicide." While a fourth letter penned after he had confessed to a priest in prison and asked for absolution recalled, "We said a prayer. He said in God's eyes I am forgiven and he will look after everyone who realises their sins. It is those who do not repent who will not be allowed into the kingdom."

> **" ...maybe it's the medication. I probably have done it in a blackout. "**

The court also heard from pathologist, Dr Vesna Djurovic, how she prepared a report about the injuries found on Janet's body after being approached by Lancashire Police.

Det Supt Graham Gooch, sent her a summary of the evidence, a record of Greenwood's taped interview and other documents, including a Home Office pathologist's report. She said she found bruises on Janet's face consistent with it being gripped with a hand over her mouth and other marks were caused by punches. Patterned bruises and abrasions to her head were consistent with stamping by a shod foot. Questioned by Mr Reid, she agreed that in his police interview Greenwood had said he held Janet by the shoulder and had put a hand over her mouth. He also spoke of punching her and kicking her the same number of times, and Dr Djurovic said that the findings agreed with that. She told the trial the diagram of Janet's injuries drawn for police by Greenwood was fully consistent with Janet's actual injuries.

Defence lawyers pointed towards the violent relationship Janet had endured with ex-boyfriend, 'The Pitbull', who was known to be out in Preston on the night she was killed. During what was a violent relationship, he had once kicked and punched her to the ground on the streets of Preston, knocking out some of her teeth. When police searched his house they found underwear with a small bloodstain. DNA tests would reveal the blood belonged to the murder victim.

Greenwood's team also suggested purse thief Raymond Hayes could be considered a suspect because he had taken some of Janet's belongings. The tactic was to put doubt in the minds of the jury despite both men having alibis at the time of the murder. In a grim irony 'The Pitbull' had phoned Janet's home at 1.41am from a pay phone more than a mile from the murder scene. At the very time she was being beaten on the riverbank.

They also pointed to psychiatric evidence that Greenwood was the kind of man who could seek to escape from his lonely, depressed existence by gaining notoriety and telling police he killed Janet when in fact he had not. He was, after all, a man with no history of violence. Despite the massive police inquiry there was absolutely no evidence pointing to Greenwood until, as one of his defence told the court, "he walks in off the street and starts singing" three years later.

On October 24, 2002, following over 13 hours of deliberations, the jury of nine women and three men were discharged after failing to reach a majority verdict. The jury forewoman told trial judge Mr Justice Leveson there was no prospect of them reaching a verdict. A date was set for a retrial the following June – seven years after the murder.

This time the jury at Liverpool Crown Court did return a verdict.

On June 30, 2003 Greenwood was cleared of murder, but found guilty of manslaughter by a ten to one majority. He was sentenced to eight years. Greenwood's legal team immediately began preparing for an appeal.

> **"** ...Greenwood was cleared of murder, but found guilty of manslaughter... **"**

Judge Mr Justice Holland had ruled jurors in the second trial should not be told about the violent ex-boyfriend with the blood stained underwear, or the purse thief who had kept secret his encounter with Janet for four years, despite the high profile appeals for any information from people who may have seen the part-time police worker on the night of her death – men Greenwood's team believed the jury should have been able to consider as potential suspects. The case was passed to the Court of Appeal, in London, to consider.

On May 28, 2004, three high court judges agreed with Greenwood's lawyers that the verdict could not be considered a safe one. Lord Justice Waller ruled, "It cannot have been right to take away from the jury's consideration all aspects of the ex-boyfriend, including that he had been the victim's boyfriend and had acted violently to her in the past and indeed was in the vicinity on the evening of her murder. It seems to us impossible to hold that this conviction was safe."

Greenwood was released from jail, his name cleared. A statement issued the same day by Lancashire Police said, "We are aware of the court's decision today to release Andrew Greenwood. We will not be looking for anyone else in connection with Janet's murder and we will not be pursuing any more evidence against Andrew Greenwood."

Today the investigation is officially listed as an undetected murder and the evidence is periodically reviewed for new leads. Two years after he was cleared of murder, on the 10th anniversary of Janet's death Greenwood would speak publically for the first time since his conviction was quashed, telling the *Lancashire Evening Post* he had been the victim of a "travesty of justice".

For Janet's family and friends, that search for justice for the confident and out going young woman with everything to live for may never be resolved.

CHAPTER ELEVEN

Welcome to the House of Horrors

Lynsey Quy, Southport, December 17, 1998

WITH just ten days to go before Christmas, Lynsey Quy was determined it was going to be a happy one for her two young children. After a year of misery, she wanted the youngsters to enjoy the kind of laughter filled festive season she remembered from her own childhood. As she made preparations for the big day, Lynsey was also secretly finalising more pressing plans for the future. The New Year was to bring a new life and so end three years of unrelenting torment at the hands of the man she once loved.

Lynsey Wilson was just 17 when she met Mitchell Quy. He was 19 and worked as a croupier at the Stanley Casino on Southport's elegant Lord Street shopping parade. Her older brother, Peter Wilson, was employed as a valet at the casino and the two men struck up a friendship. The pair would meet up after work with Quy popping round to Peter's home where he lived with his father, Peter, and mum, Linda. But it quickly became apparent that it was not just Peter he was hoping to see on his visits to the Wilson family home.

Lynsey was pregnant from a previous relationship when Quy plucked up the courage to ask her out on a date. Tall, slim and always immaculately turned out, the teenager fell head over heels for the charming older man. In August 1995, within five weeks of their first date, the couple were married.

Lynsey's parents were unhappy at the whirlwind wedding and never warmed to Quy, believing their daughter was tying the knot on the rebound from her last relationship. A short time later the pretty brunette gave birth to a daughter, Robyn. The couple's bliss should have been complete. But in the first flush of what was still a fledgling romance the young newlywed caught a glimpse of a more sinister side to her husband's openly charming veneer.

The petite teenager had never failed to draw the admiring glances of would be suitors with her bubbly personality and freckly smile. A smart and attractive young woman, she carried an air of confidence earned from her job as a barmaid. Although prone to occasional fits of adolescent pique, her big-hearted nature made her a popular figure among her family and friends. But this popularity drew increasing jealousy from her husband and the couple would argue over Quy's insecurities about his wife.

For Lynsey's part she simply loved him, and while she could not comprehend his raging envy she would not back down in the face of an argument. Quy became obsessed with the idea that she was carrying on with other men and would storm off drinking around Southport's pubs and clubs leaving her home alone with Robyn. In a twisted reaction to his own fears about his wife's fidelity, Quy took to cheating on his wife. In his perverse logic picking up women was 'revenge' for the attention Lynsey would receive. If he failed to pick up women in the resort's nightspots then he would return to the couple's rented flat to drunkenly abuse his young wife.

As the months passed the rows would become more frequent and increasingly violent. Such was his mental state that twice during their first year of married life, he was driven to attempting suicide. On one occasion he took an overdose of painkillers while at his sister-in-law's house in what was seen as a classic cry for help. He had to be admitted to Southport and Formby District General Hospital for treatment. Another time he walked away from the edge after threatening to jump from the roof of the car park on top of the Morrison's supermarket in the heart of Southport town centre. By September 1996 the couple had split up. Lynsey instigated divorce proceedings and underwent an abortion. When Quy found out about the termination he was furious. It was something he never forgave her for. And yet by the end of the year Lynsey was pregnant again with their first child together. But despite carrying his unborn baby, the pregnancy was dogged by screaming matches that by now had turned to violence.

In February 1997 the couple had an almighty bust up in the early hours of the morning. Neighbours watched in horror as Quy smashed every item in their Boundary Road home. At one point he was seen in the garden hurling rocks at the window and shouting obscenities. He then ran back inside and hurled a television set through the front window. Lynsey had dashed into the road clutching Robyn and was screaming for help. One neighbour was so concerned he captured the whole row on video. But still they stayed together and in the summer of 1997, their baby Jack was born.

The pattern of abuse continued to repeat itself, with Quy blowing up, storming off, then expressing remorse for his actions and pleading for forgiveness. Often the rows would revolve around money. When the Giro cheque arrived, Quy would disappear for two days and spend the money. Lynsey was left at home with the kids and was frequently forced to telephone her parents to ask to borrow money.

The Wilsons were worried sick for their daughter. They had seen at first hand the volatile nature of their relationship at family gatherings, when the slightest thing would see them flare up. One time when they turned up to visit the couple, Lynsey answered the door, "Welcome to the House of Horrors." The greeting was to prove horrifically prophetic.

It was during this period that Merseyside Police's domestic violence unit first became aware of the couple. In February 1998 they split up, and he was charged with incitement to cause his wife grievous bodily harm and incitement to cause criminal damage. It was claimed that Quy had asked two people to beat up his 5ft 1in wife after another ferocious row. The charges were subsequently dropped by the Crown Prosecution Service on the grounds of insufficient evidence.

Lynsey sought to legally end the marriage for a second time but her attempt failed when a family court judge refused to issue a decree absolute because the couple was still cohabiting. He advised that if the Quys wanted to go through with the divorce they would have to restart the process all over again. Terrified and unsure what to do, Lynsey turned to a women's support group in the resort for help. She was given a personal attack alarm and Quy was banned from having contact with Robyn and Jack.

Lynsey Quy.

With the support group's assistance, Lynsey set up home with her children in Birkdale. The cramped semi-detached house at 22 Stamford Road was a far cry from the million-pound mansions, Premiership footballers and championship golf course which have made the district one of the most sought after parts of the North West. But it was chance for Lynsey and her two little children to make a fresh start. For a while it worked and she even starting seeing a new man. But Quy would not let go.

The two-bedroom property was poorly lit with small windows making it quite gloomy inside. The furniture was assembled from second hand stores but it was always neat and tidy. After discovering where his estranged family was living he turned on the charm and pleaded with Lynsey for one last chance. In one note he wrote:

> I am sorry for everything that has happened over the last 14 months.
> I have put you through hell. I am sorry. I know you have heard that a million times before.
> You have been really good to me and I know I have been a shit.

When Lynsey split up with her new boyfriend, Quy made his move and managed to sweet talk her into giving him another chance. He moved into Stamford Road but after an initial period of calm, it was not long before the rows began again. This time his beatings spiralled out of control, culminating with Quy raping his wife in the living room as the children looked on. It was the final straw.

Lynsey contacted a local solicitor to arrange an appointment to start divorce proceedings. The 21-year-old dreamed of leaving behind the town where she had been born and spent all of her short life. Although she had never travelled further than Blackpool and did not even possess a passport, she set her heart on taking the children to live in Cornwall. It was just about as far away from Southport, with its fading Victorian charm, as it was possible to get within the UK. A date was set for Lynsey to see her solicitor on December 15, 1998.

Lynsey Quy had always been the responsible one in their marriage. As a teenage mum she was forced to grow up quickly. While many of her contemporaries were off at university she was bringing up two small children and wrestling with the running the family home. By now Mitchell Quy had lost his job at the casino, and the 23-year-old had made no great effort to find other means of paying the bills. It was up to Lynsey to keep the bailiffs away while struggling to provide as good a home as possible for Robyn and Jack. Some task, given the abusive nature of her husband.

As she checked the finances for Christmas, Lynsey noticed a social security cheque had not arrived. She telephoned the benefits office at 2pm on December 14 to check what had happened to the missing money and to explain how pressing it was that the money should arrive in time for the festive season. Lynsey could have saved herself the cost of the phone call. Quy had intercepted the cheque and attempted to cash it and pocket the money for himself. In an act of typical selfishness, the cash would help him enjoy a Christmas drink rather than provide some much needed cheer for his family. When staff at the benefits office told Lynsey the cheque had been dispatched, she decided to wait another day for it to arrive.

On December 15 the postman came and left without leaving the brown envelope and she quizzed her husband as to whether he had seen it. True to form, a furious row erupted. Sick of his abuse Lynsey informed Quy of her plans to leave him after Christmas and the secret meeting with a solicitor. She told him her idea

> **Lynsey informed Quy of her plans to leave him...**

was to move a long way away and that he would never see the children again. Rather than stop him in his tracks, the revelation sent him further into a blind rage. From previous experience Quy knew Lynsey was capable of carrying out her threat and he snapped. He grabbed his tiny wife by the throat and pinned her to the floor.

She had no chance.

For 20 minutes he tightened his grip as the life slowly ebbed out of the young mother. As he strangled her a single tear rolled from one of her eyes as he continued to squeeze and squeeze. It was 1am and they had been rowing for hours but this time it had come to a horrific and tragic end. After realising what he had done Quy panicked and attempted to resuscitate his wife. When he failed he briefly considered dialling 999 but could not bring himself to face the consequences of his brutal actions. As the children slept in the next room he dragged their mother's body to the couple's bedroom and sealed the doors with towels to stop any smell escaping. The following morning he calmly helped them get dressed and made their breakfast before dropping them off at nursery. As Lynsey's body lay in the marital bed he plotted what to do next. Then he turned to the one person he knew he could trust.

When his parents separated, Quy and his brother Elliot had lived with their mother until she died of cancer in his early teenage years. Throughout this time he remained in contact with his father, Michael, who lived just a few miles away. He also forged a close relationship with Elliot brought together by the tragedy and upheaval they had endured as children.

Elliot now lived alone in bedsit in Southport's Albany Road, among the cheap bed and breakfasts accommodation in the back streets off the Promenade. Lynsey had felt a little sorry for her brother-in-law and would help with his cleaning and cook him meals. On her last Christmas Day she invited him round to share a meal with her husband and their children. It was Elliot who first learned of the tragic events of the early hours of December 16. Quy turned up at his brother's house with Robyn and Jack shortly after Elliot returned home from work. Calmly he confessed to killing Lynsey just hours before. Elliot suggested his brother contact the police and admit to what he had done, but Mitchell dismissed the idea stating he could not face a future behind bars unable to see his children.

As the younger sibling Elliot had always looked up to his elder brother. But he was also aware of his violent side. As a child he had suffered from learning difficulties and was teased and bullied by his confident and out going elder brother. Whether it was through misguided loyalty or out of fear over what a man who had just confessed to a savage murder could do, Elliot agreed to help. Three days after the killing he turned up at Stamford Road and together the two men carried Lynsey's corpse into the loft while they decided what to do next.

The Quy brothers. Elliot Quy (left), helped his brother, Mitchell, dispose of his sister-in-law's body.

If Lynsey's murder had been wicked, then the plan cooked up by Mitchell Quy next was pure evil.

Five days after her murder Elliot, a butcher, made the short journey from his home in Church Street to his brother's house as planned. In a bag at his side was a hacksaw, a hammer, a screwdriver and a carpet knife. With the children asleep in the next room, they lifted the body from the roof space and dumped it in the bath. Elliot then stood in the cramped bathroom and held black bin bags open while his brother cut up his wife's body and threw in the dismembered parts.

First they removed the head and hands to make identification through fingerprints or dental records impossible. Then followed the arms and legs, as each bag was tightly bound with tape to allow no trace of their grisly contents to escape. For several hours Quy carried out his grisly task before the brothers set about removing all trace of Lynsey's blood from the bath with bleach. Now a fully fledged accomplice in the crime Elliot shrugged off the reticence he had voiced a couple of days earlier and agreed to help dispose of the severed body parts. The brothers swore a wicked pact of silence and to never tell the other where they had disposed of the body parts.

Elliot took away his sister-in-law's head and hands and left them outside a nearby grocery shop with bags of rubbish on his way home. Mitchell took responsibility for the legs, body and arms. Under the cover of darkness he carried the torso to Princes Park close to Southport's recently rebuilt pier. There he buried his grisly bundle in a shallow grave close to a rollercoaster in the overgrown shrubs that marked the boundary of the resort's Pleasureland theme park. Her arms and legs were later found wrapped in plastic bags just yards apart, in undergrowth on an embankment alongside the Liverpool to Southport railway line, close to Banastre Road in Birkdale.

Then, in an act of unbelievable wickedness, Quy took the children with him on his mission to dispose of his wife's limbs, keeping them hidden in Jack's pushchair. Robyn later told her grandmother she remembered her daddy throwing parcels over a wall when they were out for a walk. It was to be 18 months before their discovery, following a startling web of deceit created by the Quy brothers and lead by Mitchell.

After dumping Lynsey's remains he pressed ahead with his plans for a 'family' Christmas with the children. New Year celebrations came and went, and his macabre secret remained intact. If anyone asked how Lynsey was or remarked they had not seen her for a while Quy always had an excuse ready to trip off his tongue. It was not until February 1999 that the authorities became interested in her whereabouts and his cunning fell under the spotlight. Concerned that they had not seen Lynsey all year, nursery staff at daughter Robyn's school alerted the police.

When officers turned up on his doorstep, Quy was prepared for them. He explained how they had an argument and, on Christmas Day, Lynsey simply "upped and left him" taking with her just a suitcase full of clothes. In a statement he claimed his wife had gone out with a friend on Christmas Eve leaving him at home with the children. Warming to his theme, Quy described how she arrived home at 7am on Christmas Day, "totally out of her face" through drinking, and went straight to bed. About 2pm she got up, got dressed, put her make-up on and went out.

Then in an act of calculated spitefulness he accused the doting mother of ignoring Robyn as she tried to show off her new toys as she swept out of the house. In a final embellishment he claimed Lynsey came back a few days later to collect some belongings but refused to say where she had been. Police were not convinced by his story and neither were Lynsey's worried family. Whatever barbs the killer wanted to throw at his wife, accusations that she was a bad mother fell well wide of the mark. On February 17, detectives invited Quy to appear before the media at a press conference at Southport police station. Aware of the suspicion and rumour swirling around Southport journalists asked him to comment on local gossip.

He replied: "People have said things but obviously I'm going to get that. I see people talking when I walk down the street or when I go into shops. Overall, people have been very supportive. I think she's run off with another fellow. I just wish she'd get in touch. The kids are missing her. We just want to know she is okay."

> **❝ I think she's run off with another fellow. I just wish she'd get in touch. ❞**

The fiction that his wife had eloped with another man was one that Quy would develop over the following 14 months. He told police he had seen Lynsey three times round Southport after she left home, sporting a new haircut. Twice he spotted her in a black Mercedes being driven by a man and she had even smiled as it sped past. On another occasion he claimed to have seen her shopping in the resort. Quy rang police to say a note from his wife had arrived. He also said she had called home and collected some more clothes. Experts quickly established the note was a forgery and the missing clothes had been dumped by Quy.

For his next attempt to dupe police, he telephoned a local newspaper to say he had received an anonymous letter purporting to be from a woman who claimed that Lynsey had run off to Spain with her husband. Forensic tests showed this letter was also a fake. Posters were circulated throughout Southport with Lynsey's pretty face smiling from shop windows, pubs and noticeboards throughout the town. Throughout this time Quy would take Robyn and Jack to their nursery every day, revelling in the attention from young mums who eyed him with pity.

On March 19 police turned up unannounced at his house. Officers spent almost six hours combing the property and left with several bags of items for further tests. Nothing of significance was discovered but 24 days later detectives arrested Quy on suspicion of murder. He was questioned, kept overnight but only charged with incitement to cause grievous bodily harm to Lynsey during February 1998. The charges related to the complaints she had made 12 months earlier that her husband had threatened to have her beaten up. Inevitably the case grabbed the attention of the national media.

After the police press conference, Quy initially shunned requests for media interviews. But within weeks he gave an interview to a local newspaper and seemed buoyed when it appeared on the front page. After that his outlook changed and, revelling in the attention, he was interviewed on regional television news.

Next Granada TV's *Crime File* filmed a reconstruction with a lookalike cast as Lynsey, and he even joined Richard and Judy on the sofa of their daytime chat show. He calmly told morning television viewers how much he wished his missing Lynsey would return home. Then looking straight into the camera, ashen faced, he made a plea for her to get in touch.

Every time his story was the same: he had no knowledge of his wife's whereabouts, she had walked out on her children and had never cared about them. Reporters remarked that he would always look them in the eye, unblinking, as he reeled off his mantra of the temperamental wife and the long-suffering husband. But he would also quiz the journalists on what developments they knew of, searching out any bits of information on the police investigation which would help give him the upper hand. Clearly the police were telling their chief suspect nothing.

Emboldened by the failure of police to nail him, Quy became ever more cocky as he embroidered his tissue of lies. He took to goading officers, playing the part of the innocent husband harassed by detectives who had failed to find any trace of his missing wife. He would brag of his intention to sue Merseyside Police for wrongful arrest and imprisonment. His brazen contempt for detectives saw him send one officer a Christmas card with a bottle of hair dye and a note saying he should 'get rid of the grey bits to have extra confidence'. Few were taken in by his behaviour as he became obsessed with the media attention, captivated by the thrill of granting a disbelieving audience an insight into his suffering.

Away from the microphones, his grief did not prevent him from cruising Southport's nightspots to pick up women. Neighbours remarked on the steady stream of different women Quy would be seen with. Always smartly turned out, the bespectacled charmer even persuaded one or two to slip between the sheets of the bed where his dead wife had lain, waiting

" Neighbours remarked on the steady stream of different women Quy would be seen with. "

to be chopped up the previous Christmas. He even joked about how people suspected him of being a killer as his chat up lines turned up the sympathy. When police asked Quy for the name of Lynsey's dentist he remarked to a neighbour "Doesn't look good does it?" The request was significant. Lynsey had been suffering from severe toothache at the time she went missing and had fixed an appointment with her dentist for December 16, an appointment she never made.

When Quy was approached by Granada Television who asked if they could record a documentary about his plight he readily agreed. Camera crews followed him around for several months, filming him at home and out with his children. His T-shirts and trainers would always be spotlessly clean for the cameras while Robyn and Jack were equally well presented. At one point he was captured holding up a pot of wilted flowers claiming it was the last gift he had given his wife before she 'vanished'. With tears pouring down his cheeks he said: "I don't want to get rid of them. It just doesn't seem right getting rid of them." But true to form he used the filming as another opportunity to mock the police.

"They're clutching at straws. I just can't walk out there with people looking at me thinking I've done something like that to my wife. Have you any idea what that feels like?" he says.

Throughout this charade his loyal brother Elliot was playing his part to keep up the pretence. Five times, he gave investigating officers statements claiming his sister-in-law was still alive.

Without any evidence to suggest otherwise, police publically stated they were treating the case as a missing person investigation. But within weeks of Lynsey being reported missing officers had begun the task of searching for a body. A 20-strong team of specialist officers combed marshland a couple of hundred yards from the Quy family home, using sniffer dogs. A patch of land on the edge of Christ the King School's playing field, a small lake close to Southport and Formby District

General Hospital, nearby sewers and woodland in west Lancashire were all scoured.

By the summer Merseyside Police had embarked on the largest search ever carried out by the force. Search teams dragged Southport's Marine Lake, probed the concrete foundations of the recently-constructed Traumatizer fairground ride in Pleasureland after rumours swirled around Southport that Lynsey's remains had been dumped in the 50ft pits excavated for the steelwork. RAF jets were drafted in to fly over Southport with high-resonance cameras to look for any evidence of a buried body.

British Transport police officers search alongside railway lines near Southport, Merseyside, for the remains of Lynsey Quy.

Detectives searched the couple's home on three occasions. During the third search they employed military experts armed with an X-ray machine similar to the one used to look for missing IRA victims in Ireland. The equipment was able to penetrate deep through earth or concrete to establish if there was anything under there which could indicate the presence of a body. It was so sensitive that it was capable of detecting minute traces of human remains such as tissue, blood or bone fragments, and was used to electronically scan floorboards and the couple's back garden. Excavators carried out a deep search of a landfill site on Bentham Way close to Stamford Road after consulting with forensic psychologists and the specialist police computer database Catchem. The computer has logged every murder committed in Britain over the past 30 years and pinpointed the rubbish tip as a possible location for Lynsey's body. All to no avail.

By June 1999 the police publically admitted they were treating Lynsey's disappearance as murder. Detective Superintendent Geoff Sloan, the man at the head of the inquiry, told reporters: "She could walk in tomorrow, but I'm 99.9 per cent sure she is dead. Mr Quy is a valid suspect. He is the person who had the last sighting and the opportunity and motive. She was going to go ahead with the divorce proceedings and that would have been a valid reason to kill her."

If he did not know before, Quy was left in no doubt he was the prime suspect. But the lack of a breakthrough only encouraged him to hit back by stepping up his taunting of detectives. His response was to invite reporters into his back garden and announce, "I think they have hit a dead end. All they want to do is put pressure on me. At first it did really get me down, but I have got nothing to hide. The police said at one point they were thinking about taking the search international. I think rather than digging holes and going through lakes they should widen it. It's like they have given up the thought of finding her alive but there has not really been a nationwide appeal for her. I think they should broaden their horizons."

As Robyn's fourth birthday approached in September 1999, he brazenly admitted he would give up all hope if Lynsey failed to send a card or present to her daughter. He was toying with police and reveling in what for him was a high stakes game. For Peter and Linda Wilson, the disappearance of their beloved daughter was anything but a game.

The couple were living apart in Birkdale when Lynsey went missing, but her disappearance brought them back together. From day one they never believed Quy's version of events but were forced to remain on civil terms with the killer for the sake of their grandchildren. Displaying amazing self-restraint, they would go round to Stamford Road to pick up Robyn and Jack whenever they could. As Peter would later admit, "I was convinced from day one that he had killed her and it was difficult to live with that, difficult to control yourself and not to do something about it."

" I was convinced from day one that he had killed her... "

Small comfort arrived in June 1999 in the form of a letter of sympathy from the Queen. But the Wilsons did not sit back and wait for developments. In every spare hour they would head out and put up 'missing' posters, carrying out their own heartbreaking search for any trace of Lynsey. The Wilsons' elder daughter, Paula, and husband, Roy Houghton, bought a minibus, rakes and trowels and in evenings and at weekends the family searched wasteland, countryside, lakes and ponds in Southport. They would wade into ponds with sticks and spend hours prodding around for their daughter's body. The couple bought a map of Southport and would mark off the areas they had scoured for any trace of Lynsey. Each weekend relatives would meet for Sunday dinner and afterwards discuss where they would take their search next. Among the people who offered them support and advice was Marie McCourt, the mother of Helen McCourt, who was murdered in Billinge and her body never recovered. The Wilsons would pay psychics for any clue which could help end their agony. Famed psychic Uri Geller, after they contacted him by e-mail, invited them to his Berkshire home the very next

Lynsey's father Peter carries out his own heartbreaking search for his daughter.

day. The television personality was very sympathetic and, after studying clothes belonging to Lynsey, he told the couple he knew she was dead. Geller predicted that her body would be found very near water but not in it. Studying a map of Southport he pinpointed a spot between Pleasureland and the Marine Lake very close to where Lynsey's torso would later be unearthed. Eerily, Geller said he was receiving mixed signals as to her true resting place.

In April 2000 Det Supt Geoff Sloan was asked to carry out a thorough review of the case. Among the facts nagging detectives was the missing benefits cheque. Why would Lynsey report it missing if she was planning to run away? Why had her cash card not been used since the day the cheque went missing? Surely these were not the actions of someone who needed the money for Christmas. And what of the dental appointment she missed? Given that she was in severe pain would she really have failed to turn up?

A behavioural expert was called in to look at the interviews Quy had given to police and to study his quotes to the media. Police were keen to analyse his

Lynsey Quy was finally at rest.

responses to lines of questioning, to enable them to build an interview strategy around predicting his likely answers. After weeks of studying the evidence, Det Supt Sloan decided police had enough to arrest Mitchell Quy again. This time he would be charged with murder. Within hours Quy's calm exterior was shattered and he began to tell everything he knew admitting he had "over reacted" when Lynsey revealed her intention to divorce him. He passed a handwritten note to a custody officer, stating:

> **❝ This time he would be charged with murder. ❞**

> *The person who conspired with me to dispose of Lynsey's body was Elliot, my brother. My father had nothing to do with it. He does not know what happened.*

When confronted by police with Mitchell's confession, Elliot detailed the horrifying secret of how the brothers had disposed of Lynsey's body. By the time detectives returned to speak Mitchell again he had drawn a diagram detailing where his wife's limbs and torso had been dumped. Handcuffed and under tight security he was driven around the different spots pointing out the exact areas where he had hidden the body parts.

The brothers' father Michael Quy was arrested on suspicion of conspiring to pervert the course of justice. But the case against him was dismissed by the Crown Prosecution Service through lack of evidence.

Officers were then handed the heartbreaking task of breaking the news to Peter and Linda Wilson. Bravely Peter spoke to reporters: "From when Lynsey was first reported missing I knew there would never be a happy outcome. From day one I knew something terrible had happened. I tried to prepare for this but it's worse

LANCASHIRE
Evening Post

FINAL

JOBS BOOSTER
Page 3

WEBSITE: lancashireeveningpost.co.uk

WEDNESDAY, JUNE 14, 2000

25p

QuidsIn FOR THE BEST DEALS IN THE COUNTY... PAGE 9 TONIGHT

Camera Cuties VOTE FOR THE CUTEST KID IN LANCASHIRE

SCOTTISH RIVALS FOR PNE'S NO. 1 TARGET SPORT

PRESTON NORTH END

LYNSEY SEARCH: TORSO IS DUG UP

GRIM SEARCH: Police scour wasteland in the hunt for evidence after human remains were found

POLICE in Southport searching for the body of missing mother of two Lynsey Quy are set to widen the search after finding a torso.

Detectives announced they had made the grim find at a site in Prince's Park.

They revealed her husband Mitchell, who has protested his innocence and has been charged with her murder, is cooperating with

By ALAN BURROWS

the police in their search. Police targeted a 20m stretch behind the go-kart track at Pleasureland, which was recently covered in rubble and top soil by contractors.

Detectives, using a mechanical digger and a scientific support vehicle, drilled bore holes to allow a sniffer dog to detect human remains.

Frogmen from the underwater search team also trawled the Marine Lake in

search of a knife but police today announced that searches in the artificial lake and by the fair were complete.

Intensive

A police spokesman said: "Detectives are continuing to make intensive efforts to recover the outstanding human remains.

"Searching at the site by Merseyside Police officers using specially-trained dogs has now ended.

"The searches being car-

ried out in Southport are now winding down."

Police found a woman's right leg by a railway line in Birkdale on Friday night and a left leg was found nearby on Saturday afternoon.

Lynsey 21, vanished from the home she shared with husband Mitchell, 25, and their two children at Christmas 1998.

Last week, three men, including Mitchell, were arrested following an 18-month investigation.

LYNSEY QUY: Vanished from home at Christmas 1998

CROSSWORD: Page 12 LETTERS: Page 14 TV: Pages 20-21 CLASSIFIED: Pages 23-38 SPORT: Pages 39-44 CONTACT US: 01772 254841

than I ever imagined it would be. It's like a nightmare. We used to ring him and ask him where Lynsey was and he used to say, 'I don't know where she is'. I never liked Mitchell from the start. He has done nothing since the beginning but blacken Lynsey's name. We will never get over what's happened."

❝ I never liked Mitchell from the start. ❞

But, despite his grief, Peter also thanked police for their efforts in searching for his daughter. He said: "I would like to thank Merseyside Police, every officer involved, no matter how minutely, for what they have done."

On January 16, 2001 Mitchell Quy was jailed for life at Liverpool Crown Court.

Trial judge Mr Justice Leveson told him, "You murdered her, cut up her body and distributed it in various places. You then embarked on a deception of breathtaking cynicism, bemoaning your wife's absence, castigating the police for directing their attentions towards you. The callous disregard for your wife's body and those concerned in her welfare and the way in which you led her child to believe her mother had abandoned her was just evil." He was later told he would not be considered for parole for 17 years.

Jailed for life: wife-killer Mitchell Quy.

Six days later Elliot was jailed for seven years for helping to dispose of his sister-in-law's body. Hundreds of mourners turned out for Lynsey's funeral at Holy Trinity Church, in Southport. Many had never met the young mother-of-two but were touched by her plight in a crime which scarred the seaside resort. One explained her reasons for being at the church, "I just wanted to come along. I am in my early 20s and have young children like Lynsey. I read all the newspaper stories about her and I wanted to pay my respects and say goodbye. It's tragic."

Alice Pritchard, a close friend of Lynsey, read a poem composed in her memory entitled 'Memories of Lynsey'. She told the packed church, "When I think of Lynsey and the friendship we shared I remember the line of a poem I learned at school. That is, 'a thing of beauty is a joy forever for it will never fade into nothingness'. You had a beautiful smile and you were a wonderful mummy."

Lynsey's tearful family left the church in a solemn procession as the Bette Midler song 'Wind Beneath My Wings' was played at the end of the half-hour service. Her mother Linda had chosen the song as it was the theme tune from her daughter's favourite film *Beaches*. Lynsey's ashes were scattered in Cornwall, the haven where she dreamed of beginning a new life, away from the evil clutches Mitchell Quy.

Other Local Titles Available from At Heart:

Lancashire's Four Seasons

From the majestic sweep of Morecambe Bay to the foothills of the Pennines Lancashire is blessed with some of the finest scenery in all of Britain. Lancashire's Four Seasons captures the essence of the Red Rose county in all of its majesty.

£12.99   ISBN: 978-1-84547-183-5

Blackpool Then & Now

This fascinating book from The Blackpool Gazette takes you back in time to the good old days, to reveal how famous landmarks as well as the town's less familiar corners have been transformed. Blackpool Then & Now forms a lasting souvenir of the resort's history.

£12.95   ISBN: 978-1-84547-153-8

Legends: The Great Players of Blackpool FC

Thirty Blackpool FC players will be forever remembered as the true greats of Bloomfield Road. Legends comprises of profiles, statistics and action photographs of Blackpool FC's greatest players. Delve inside to find the fans' favourites from throughout the decades.

£12.99   ISBN: 978-1-84547-182-8

Preston North End 1954 FA Cup Final   Mike Hill

Preston North End's march to Wembley for the 1954 FA Cup Final has gone down in history among followers of the famous old team. This fascinating record revives memories of a golden era of post war football and an occasion still fondly remembered by football lovers today.

£12.99   ISBN: 978-1-84547-171-2

Garstang Past

In 2007, the Garstang Courier published its eight hundredth "Reverent Reflections" article by popular columnist, Canon Ron Greenall. Garstang Past is a tribute and thanks to readers of the newspaper who have contributed to the column and to the people of Garstang, both past and present.

£12.99   ISBN: 978-1-84547-137-8

For more information or to buy any of these titles, visit **www.atheart.co.uk**
or your local bookseller